# STORIES OF
# HOPE
# AND
# HUMOR

# STORIES OF HOPE AND HUMOR

*To James
With love
Donia Caspersen Crouch*

## DONIA CASPERSEN CROUCH

TATE PUBLISHING
AND ENTERPRISES, LLC

Published by Tate Publishing & Enterprises, LLC
127 E. Trade Center Terrace | Mustang, Oklahoma 73064 USA
1.888.361.9473 | www.tatepublishing.com

Tate Publishing is committed to excellence in the publishing industry. The company reflects the philosophy established by the founders, based on Psalm 68:11,
*"The Lord gave the word and great was the company of those who published it."*

Book design copyright © 2013 by Tate Publishing, LLC. All rights reserved.
*Cover design by Rodrigo Adolfo*
*Cover photo by Lindsey Miller Crouch*
*Author photo by Angela Antonson*
*Interior design by Jake Muelle*

Published in the United States of America

ISBN: 978-1-62902-532-2
1. Self-Help / Motivational & Inspirational
2. Humor / General
13.10.29

# DEDICATION

This book is dedicated to Jimmy.
I love you with all my heart.

# INTRODUCTION

This collection of essays was first published in a small Texas newspaper. It was a dream come true when Roger Cowles, editor of the Port Arthur News gave me space for a weekly column. "What do you want to write about?" he asked.

"Family," I answered quickly. Life with thirteen brothers and sisters and an effervescent Momma has generated plenty of writing material. Recently, Momma and I scribbled the names of her ever expanding tribe on a piece of paper. Counting kids, grandkids, great grandkids and sons and daughters-in-law, the number approached 100. There are more babies on the way.

The faces on the book's cover are those of our first grandchild, Daniel Shepherd Crouch, and his loyal sidekick, Woody Harrelson. Shep's mom, Lindsey captured this moment. Of all the photos we considered for the cover, this one best reflects the whimsical way of family life.

I have always gotten a kick out of family stories. I hope you do, too!

# TABLE OF CONTENTS

# A CRAZY CROWDED CHRISTMAS

I'll admit it. Christmas Eve at my mother's house can be intimidating. With 65 people of all ages and sizes, the living area is jam packed. At first, before everyone has settled into couches and chairs, it's hard to get in the front door. Approximately 50 of these people share my DNA so I think it's a blast to be in their midst. My husband does not love it quite so much.

This year, while elbowing my way toward the dining room table for a bowl of chili, I considered how things might look through my husband's eyes. It's sensory overload: teenaged cousins screaming with glee and "too tired" toddlers whining for one more cookie. People bumping into each other all over the place, greeting each other with hugs and kisses. For Jimmy, it's too loud, too crazy and too crowded.

He doesn't understand why we continue to gather at my mother's house. Even though our parents raised 14 kids there, it's not big enough. The Fire Marshall would not approve. For years, siblings with larger homes have offered to host the evening. Momma won't hear of it. "This could be my last Christmas," she says with a twinkle in her blue eyes. At 88, her power of persuasion is as strong as ever.

And so it's the same every year. We gather at 5pm for Mass. Father Bill blesses us with a home liturgy and we sing, mostly off-key, to classics like *Joy to the*

*World* and *Silent Night.* The sacred service is followed by dinner and desserts. Everybody brings something to eat. By the time we unload our offerings, the dining room table is covered with chili, ham, brisket, salads and side dishes.

The sweets table holds cookies and cakes galore. The most popular item is served in a trifle dish. The dessert layered with pudding, devil's food cake, and whipped cream goes by the name of Charlie's Chocolate Adieu. That's to honor Daddy who died almost 25 years ago. Known for hiding Hershey kisses in his sock drawer, he passed his sweet tooth on to every one of his kids.

Christmas Eve has always been packed with people. I was so accustomed to the chaos, I didn't think to prepare my new boyfriend before meeting my family on Christmas Eve 1975. It was only our second date. Having asked him to pick me up at my parent's house, I will never forget the confused look on his face as I introduced him to one sibling after another. Understanding kicked in slowly as he scanned the 14 stockings wrapping around the mantel.

Jimmy came from a small family where holidays were ordered and controlled. It must have felt like baptism by fire to be thrown in with so many family and extended family members. We thought it was fun for one of the uncles to dress as Santa and pass out candy canes to the little kids. He was afraid he would be tapped for the job.

While I am certain that my spouse won't be wearing the beard and belt anytime soon, he now embraces the tradition like a member of the home team. I can't say when his conversion happened, but I knew it was underway when he did something that had nothing to do with Christmas. He invited my mother to live with us. She graciously declined, but she and I both knew what his invitation meant. He felt like a son to her and a brother to my siblings.

Last Christmas Eve at the end of the night, he displayed more family harmony. Momma had gone to bed and most of the revelers had gone home. Siblings and in-laws were in the kitchen, scraping pots and taking out trash. As we cleaned, we analyzed the evening. "Next year we'll move it to a bigger house," said one brother. Everyone nodded in agreement. I looked at my husband. He didn't say a thing, but his silence spoke volumes. I knew exactly what he was thinking:

*"This place is too crazy and too crowded. It's also exactly where we will be this time next year."*

# A POPE FOR THE PEOPLE

"Habemus Papum." We have a pope.

It only took two days for 115 cardinals to agree and then white smoke! I'd give anything to be in Rome during this historical event so I could feel the people's jubilation. By now, you may be tired of reading about Pope Francis. He has been all over the news since the moment he was elected. I'm going to write about him anyway. My enthusiasm for the new pontiff leaves me no choice. He seems to be having that effect on everybody.

I haven't been this pumped about a pope since I was a child. Pope John XXIII was our family's favorite. That's because we enjoyed a personal connection. It was April of 1959 and Momma and Daddy were at St. Joseph Hospital having another baby. They named him John in honor of the pope. One of the nuns from the hospital had a brother working in the Vatican. She decided to send him a letter introducing the American family who so closely followed the church's policy on birth control. Sister Eugenia wanted the pope to know he had a brand new namesake. Like Pope John XXIII, our newborn was no lightweight. Weighing in at 12 pounds, he was the biggest baby Momma ever delivered. He was her lucky thirteen.

When Momma got home from the hospital, (doctors kept postpartum patients for at least a week back then and not just those who were afraid to go home) a package was waiting on the front porch. It bore an Italian postmark. Inside were treasures: a letter of congratulations, a papal blessing and a handful of sterling silver medals. On one side was our Blessed Virgin Mary and on the other was Pope John XXIII.

It was exciting to be personally acknowledged by the global leader of the Catholic Church. Grateful as they were, Momma and Daddy couldn't help but chuckle when they took inventory. There were fourteen medals in the box, but they only had thirteen kids. A few months later our mother went for her annual checkup. It turned out that the Pope was a prophet. Momma was pregnant with number fourteen.

His framed papal blessing and picture was hung over the stairway that very day. While we never met him, Pope John XXIII was in our prayers every night. Sweet and personable, he seemed more of a grandfather than a pontiff. I think I'll soon be feeling the same way about Pope Francis. Did you see the coverage of him addressing the people in St. Peter's Square for the first time? His face radiated love and joy. The enthusiasm in the crowd gave me goose bumps. When he asked his new flock to pray for him, I knew he was special.

If I wasn't convinced that The Holy Spirit was in charge, I'd say our new Chief Shepherd has hired one heck of a screenwriter. He's only been pope for a week, but he's already carved a path to our hearts. Forgoing a limo ride to take the bus with brother cardinals and choosing to wear a silver cross instead of a more flamboyant gold one. These things show he is a pope for the people. What really got my attention was something he did long before stepping into the papal limelight.

More than ten years ago, during a hospice visit, he washed and kissed the feet of AIDS patients. Sounds like Jesus, doesn't it? We expect Catholic journalists to be singing his praises, but writers and broadcasters of all faiths seem to be embracing him. He seems to be exactly what we need right now. A leader who transcends affiliations? Someone who focuses on service and simplicity rather than power and opulence?

Everyone agrees he's done noble things, but it's his passion for the people that thrills me the most. The Vicar of Christ is tightly connected to his flock. An observer from St. Peter's Square said that when he stepped out on the balcony, he was like a little boy on Christmas morning. "Except", she said, "he opened a much bigger gift than he ever expected". In my opinion, so did we.

# A VISION IN IVORY LACE

Yesterday was a big day. My daughter and I went wedding dress shopping for the very first time. As I have only one daughter, I was extremely excited about our scouting expedition. She was thrilled, too. Having driven 7 hours from her home in another state, she didn't arrive until almost 11pm. By 11:00 the next morning we had seen enough silk, satin and taffeta to outfit every girl in town.

Ask any mother who has helped a daughter with a wedding and she'll tell you the learning curve is steep. We quickly learned that there's a certain protocol that comes with a shopping trip of this magnitude. First, the bridal dress consultant assesses the bride's general preferences such as sweetheart or V-neckline, conventional waist or empire. Then she can rule out entire categories of dresses and quickly narrow the focus. She escorts the bride and her entourage (I was thankful to be the only one in hers today) up and down the designated display racks for the purpose of selection. Our veteran saleslady suggested lugging no more than 4 at a time into the dressing room. "It's easy to get overwhelmed," she counseled.

Our daughter has always been extremely inde-pendent, so I reminded myself to keep my thoughts to myself. But early in the hunt for her gown, she made it clear that she wanted my opinion. Thrilling as it was to be invited so unrestrictedly into the decision-making process, it was also a bit daunting. Our taste in clothing is so different. We've never agreed on fashion or style. Thinking back on Saturday shopping trips in high school, the tension and conflict came back with a visceral clarity. I cringed at the thought that things might take a nasty turn in the oversized dressing rooms of this fancy bridal salon. About that time, our trusty saleslady walked in carrying a dress that neither one of us had pulled from the rack.

"Try this," she said holding up something so fluffy and feminine it would have made a fairy godmother proud. My eyes grew wide. I couldn't imagine that my "raised with 2 brothers and played catcher on the softball team" child would consider such a frilly get-up. To my surprise, she slipped into that gown like she had been waiting for it all her life. Next, she asked for a compatible veil. Regal as a queen, she lifted her chin awaiting her crown of ivory tulle. When our dark haired daughter stepped onto the platform and turned toward the mirrors, I gasped. Her image took my breath away. It's an overused expression, but truly says it all.

For one long moment, I really couldn't breathe or speak. Most *Mother of the Brides* react with a lump in their throats and tears in their eyes the first time they see their daughters dressed in white from head to toe. But it wasn't about the dress. It was about how she thought she looked in the dress. When she saw her reflection in the mirror, she looked like a 5 year old on a carousel. Her eyes sparkled and her smile lit up the room. I could feel her confidence growing.

Of course, it was a beautiful gown but then again, that could be said about most of them. It was more than that. The gown did something for her that went beyond style and fabric. I suddenly realized for the first time that it's not about how a woman looks in her wedding gown, it's how she feels when she wears it that's transforming.

With that discovery, something else became clear. I had nothing to worry about. My job as MOB was not to offer an opinion. My job was to quietly hold up the mirror so she could decide for herself. The dresses are all lovely. It doesn't matter a bit which one she chooses as long as it makes her feel like a queen while she wears it. She only needs one thing from me. It is the simple affirmation that whichever one she selects, that will be my favorite, too.

# ACCEPTANCE BRIDGES GENERATION GAP

Sometimes our kids do things our way. Sometimes they don't. When they choose a different path, it's tempting to worry over what can go wrong. I'm guessing that's what makes for the gap between generations. When I was young, I didn't understand why people from different generations saw things so differently. I'm certain I didn't know that acceptance could build be such a powerful tool in relationships. Now that I'm watching our grown children find their way in the world, I get the message loud and clear.

Let's take for example, the subject of parenthood. Our son and daughter-in-law recently shared that they are expecting. We're thrilled over the new life that is about to expand our family. It's a dream come true for all of us. When our kids first learned of their pregnancy, they wanted to know the gender as soon as possible. At first, it seemed essential in order to plan. So they scheduled an appointment for a sonogram and compared calendars for a date to announce the news to their friends. "Gender Reveal" parties are the latest thing.

That got my attention. A friend of mine once painted her nursery pink based on information gleaned from a sonogram. When her newborn showed up as a third son instead of a first daughter, she was shocked. Instead of basking in the afterglow of childbirth, she fretted over "all the pink stuff" she needed to exchange.

I didn't share that story with our children. Other people's tales of woe are never effective anyway. To my delight, some friend of a friend told them that curiosity provides extra strength for pushing. Any mother knows a woman will push like her life depends on it to get that baby out, whether she knows the gender or not. In any case, we're glad they've changed their minds. Waiting has proven to be more practical. And more fun.

I was in the middle of relaying the latest adjustment to their plan when our daughter-in-law called with another report. This time she stated they have signed up with a midwife for a home birth rather than for a doctor in a hospital. Once again, I bit my tongue and kept my opinion to myself. They are currently writing a birth plan *"to enhance the natural birthing process while focusing on safety and comfort for mother and child"*.

That quote from the brochure was the opposite of our experience. "The natural birthing process?" "A comfortable and relaxed atmosphere?" We didn't have a delivery plan. My monthly appointments were as uplifting as a 3000 mile oil change. By the 5th month, my obstetrician was in full lecture mode. I will admit to gaining a few extra pounds over and above the baby weight, but that was because of Christmas parties and fruit cake. Anyway, he didn't have to be so mean about it.

It's obvious that our daughter-in-law's midwife embraces a totally different philosophy. "Every pregnancy develops at its own pace", she says. In your face, Dr. Johnson! The more I think about it, the better it sounds. How lovely to deliver a baby in the relaxed and comfortable atmosphere of one's own home. Soothing music, aromatherapy, a woman who understands how it feels to give birth assisting... Bring it on! I'm starting to think that our kids might be on to something.

As soon as I began to embrace their seemingly radical plan, the phone rang again. "We are considering a water birth", she said. What does that mean? Please tell me there is no lake or river involved! I googled *water birth* and clicked on the first website that came up. The next thing I knew, I was watching a healthy newborn "swimming" through a water-filled tub into the arms of a waiting midwife. It was peaceful and completely drama free.

I haven't let Granddad in on the latest change of plans. I'm guessing he might need a bit more time to adjust. Perhaps that's why we call the space between generations "a gap". It takes a bridge of acceptance to get across.

# AGGIE, SOLDIER, COWBOY AND PATRIARCH

The world has lost another hero. His death didn't make national news, but the people from this neck of the woods will surely miss him. William Sanders Edwards- soldier, Aggie, cowboy and dad- passed on last week at the age of 90. He lived long and he lived well. He prospered. His list of achievements could fill a book, but raising good kids is what he cared about.

At our house, we called him Uncle Billy. He wasn't related by blood, but he married our mother's best friend and that made him family. Beaumont girls born and bred, Momma and Evie grew up sharing homework and boyfriends. They both married men from out of town and reticently left Beaumont behind. Uncle Billy moved Evie to the country while Daddy offered Momma life in the big city.

Shortly afterward, they each started cranking out babies. Fertile as the day was long, Momma finished up with 10 girls and 4 boys while Evie filled their house with almost the opposite- 9 boys and 4 girls. With so much to celebrate, we got together regularly. Huge slabs of beef on the pit, homemade cakes and plenty of potato salad. That was all we needed for a picnic in the country. Two families with 27 kids running free in the great outdoors? It was a foolproof recipe for fun.

For city kids, it was true paradise: horseback riding, trampoline bouncing, and a swimming pool. If that wasn't enough, we could hitch a ride to the back forty in an open air jeep. It seemed like anyone at the Edwards house over 12 years of age was a seasoned driver. Licenses were not required, it seemed, on country roads and pastures. What a contrast to our urban existence. The freedom was exhilarating. No wonder we loved those day trips.

After one of the Fourth of July picnics, we talked our parents into letting the older kids stay a little longer instead of caravanning home with them. When we finally rolled down the gravel driveway, a sudden change in weather caught us by surprise. The skills of our newly licensed sister were no match for the blinding rain. She managed to get us and that wood paneled station wagon a mere thirty miles down the road before giving up and pulling over. That was before cell phones. How our "knight in shining pickup truck" found us, we will never know but his headlights flashed in our rear view mirror. We knew he had come to lead us home. Not to Houston, but to the ranch. Our "aunt" and "uncle" made room for six more kids that night.

Rescuing children seemed to be Uncle Billy's forte. When he was six, our brother was the only male in our growing family of 8. Uncle Billy showed up in town one day for the express purpose of bringing him to the ranch for the summer. Blessed with 7 sons, Uncle Billy must have felt sorry for the little boy surrounded by sisters. How did he convince his wife to take in an extra when their bedrooms were already full and another baby was on the way? However he did it, Cas is sure glad he did. That's how he learned to rope and brand just like the Edwards boys.

If Uncle Billy had a bucket list, he never told us about it. He was more interested in doing things for others than himself. I guess that's how he earned 5 bronze service stars during WWII. We learned at his funeral that he was the one who got his fellow soldiers home when the army was "tapped out' at the end of the war. He was a member of The Greatest Generation. In addition to that, he cooked his kids' breakfast and got them to school on time.

He was honored for the things he did as a soldier, an Aggie, and yes, even a cowboy. But it was the effort he made as a father that brought out the best in him. His thirteen kids appreciated that. They weren't the only ones.

# BEACH LIFE BECKONS

I'm a bum.

A beach bum, that is. All I can think about when the temperature rises above 90 is getting my feet into sand and surf. Since low humidity and cool temperatures are my husband's idea of a good time, we spent our vacation in Colorado last summer. Most evenings, we watched the sun set from the hot tub on the deck. As the sun slipped over the horizon, we marveled at God's handiwork. There was purple mountain majesty coming at us from every direction.

Still, I missed the beach. When you grow up a mere hour away, it's easy to get addicted to the rolling waves. With fourteen kids, our mother needed regular breaks from her labor. She figured out early on that the hour drive was manageable even for a tribe as large as ours. On Saturdays, we packed the cars with towels and sandwiches after breakfast, spent the afternoon on the beach and still got home before dark.

If day picnics with the family were fun, weekends at my best friend's beach house were awesome. During the summers of our middle school years, we frequented the house on Bolivar peninsula. The fun began on the ferry. Waiting in a hot car to see if we'd be among the next group of vehicles to fill the big vessel seemed endless. However, once we claimed our spot on that big metal barge time flew. As soon as the captain gave the OK, we jumped out of the car clutching paper bags of stale bread. Our boat ride to the peninsula was spent tossing "seven grain" to the swooping seagulls.

With nine kids in Elizabeth's family, the house with green shutters was a crowded place. I'm sure that's why I felt so at home there. It's also why Elizabeth and I didn't get to spend as many nights on the coveted swinging bed. Everybody wanted his turn on the mattress suspended by chains. That made our time between the swaying sheets on the screened in porch all the better. We fell asleep to the roar of waves. It was heaven.

Hurricanes have blown away big sections of that beach over the past decade. Before that, we girls had enough sand to search for starfish. Every morning awakened by the sun's first light, we wriggled into our still damp and gritty swimsuits and ran down to the shoreline. Our goal was to hit the beach before the seiners (commercial fishermen) finished dragging their nets. If all went well, we brought a few crabs from their catch home with us. By the time we returned for breakfast, that night's gumbo was already simmering on the back burner. We ran right back to the beach again after devouring our scrambled eggs.

Sometimes we hung out with Elizabeth's brother-in-law on a nearby fishing pier. There were almost twenty years between us and Elizabeth's married sister. Mary Lou, with her husband and a baby added much to the mystique of my friend's wild and wonderful family. One day when Mike was trying to get a fish off of his hook, it wiggled from his grasp and landed on the pier.

He stepped on the flopping creature and ended up with a dorsal fin in the bottom of his foot. I didn't learn to fish that day, but I did learn to respect the sharp fin of a catfish.

That was a different time when there weren't so many rules. I'm not sure whether bonfires were legal even then, but I know we built them on a regular basis. The challenge was to see how high we could pile the wood and how many hours we could keep the flames going. After the fire was blazing, we sat in a circle roasting wieners and marshmallows. I longed for a seat next to Pat, Elizabeth's brother. He was ten years our senior and my first heart throb. Handsome and cocky, he was a ringer for James Dean.

Reliving these memories makes me want to get on the phone and rent a beach house. No mountains for me this summer. My vacation will be chock full of sand, surf and seaweed. Who knows? I might even catch a catfish.

# BEST PRESENTS NOT UNDER THE TREE

There are five days left until Santa's big scene. If you are among the folks who are still rushing around, you have plenty of company. Presents are on everyone's minds during the last days before Christmas. I am presently seeking the perfect thing for everyone on my list even though none of us really needs anything. Those clever television commercials can nudge anyone into a state of lust over the purchase of a new car or ring.

When pressed to recall the presents I have received in my life, I can only come up with a few. At the top of the list is the pear-shaped diamond Jimmy slipped on my finger when he asked me to marry him. That gift arrived in time for Christmas 1976. When we married a few months later, it was not a double ring ceremony. My intended declined my offer of a gold band.

I didn't mind. My father hadn't worn a wedding ring, either. Ten years later, my honey felt differently. "This is for you", he said pulling the last gift from under the tree. Inside the blue velvet box I found a man's ring engraved with these words: "*I love you more every day*". On that note, our marriage moved to a new level. Special gifts have a way of changing things.

Like that black patent dance bag I received for my 11th Christmas. Growing up in a big family left me with a need to set myself apart. The Saturday classes at Kotchetovsky's School of Dance helped with that. Most of my siblings chose sports instead of ballet. Miss Barbara Lee was the perfect combination of poise and athleticism. She taught us to hold our heads high. With her no-nonsense teaching style and perfect posture, she earned my greatest respect. She wasn't the only one to inspire me.

I worshipped the older ballerinas. Tall and slender, they monopolized the dressing room as if they were the only ones who belonged there. Prima donnas, every one, they didn't give me the time of day. I wanted to be just like them. Slipping from their blue jeans into leotards, they were butterflies shedding cocoons. In my mind, their transformations hinged on the contents of their black patent dance bags.

I absolutely had to have one. Santa did not disappoint me. With my name in gold across the front, that tote turned me into a real ballerina. Every Saturday morning, I zipped my pink ballet slippers and tutu into it and slung it over my shoulder. Being chosen for a solo was suddenly a possibility. If I looked the part and felt the part, perhaps I could dance the part. "Get out of my way, Baryshnikov!" I never did get a solo, but it was not for lack of confidence.

This past Thanksgiving, I was blessed with another life changing gift. Gathered around our Thanksgiving table, we took turns being grateful. I thanked God for our late son-in-law who had succumbed to cancer a few months before. Our daughter, his widow, expressed gratitude for the family that's helped her survive her loss. Our younger son was thankful for the job he has found.

When it was our daughter-in-law's turn, she seemed uncharacteristically tongue-tied. Her eyes were shining and her smile was bright, but she kept looking over at our son. It was as if she was asking him something. By the time he gave her the nod, we had already guessed what she was about to say. "I'm pregnant!!!!!"

Jumping up from the table, we bumped into each other. It was a "hugfest" for one and all. Congratulations persisted till the turkey got cold. The ladies wiped away tears while the guys bear-hugged and razzed the new daddy. My friend Molly's words (she has nine grandkids)came back to me. *"Grandchildren are the best. We get to play with them and send them home but I never want to send them home"*.

I've been graced with some really great gifts over the years, but the promise of a grandbaby makes the rest of them look pale by comparison. Presents make us happy. The best ones don't fit under the tree. May we all receive something this holiday season that's wrapped in nothing but love.

# SHARING TIME MAKES
# BETTER MARRIAGE

I cry every time a friend gets divorced.

It happened again last week. A dear friend of mine and her husband split up after less than two years. It was not the first marriage for either of them and they had no children together. Citing irreconcilable differences, they agreed it was neither one's fault. It just wasn't working. Still, it broke my heart when she packed up and moved out.

I find relationships fascinating. Ever since I was a little girl, marriage has seemed magical. I watched the push/ pull of my parents' interaction and wondered how they did it. Raising 14 children surely made life challenging, but their individual differences also created friction. Daddy was incredibly intense. Relationships were not easy for him. Momma is an easy going individual who enjoys everything and everybody. Without personality traits in common, it was shared values, love and strong commitment to each other that kept them together. No matter what happened, they honored their partnership.

This weekend there's a wedding shower for my niece. She is marrying a young man from a similar background. Like her, he has a college degree. Like her, he is gainfully employed. It is the first marriage for both of them and they come from intact families. On paper, their future looks promising. We shall see what the winds of daily life blow their way.

Last week, a friend who has been married for 34 years said she and her husband have started something new. They have begun to cook together. It's an effort to fortify their relationship. A workaholic, he has always had trouble finding time for her. Now, instead of watching "Late Show with David Letterman" before they turn out the lights, they read recipes from cookbooks. On Sundays, they plan and prepare a few dinners for the following week. Their new program has only been underway for a few weeks, but so far the results are encouraging. She says he has never been more affectionate.

Chopping and sautéing can enrich a decades old marriage? It sounds preposterous, but it probably doesn't matter what a couple does together as long as it is something that both enjoy. As long as it fosters harmony, right? I remember what our counselor told us at the height of our marital crisis. Relationships are like high rise buildings. By the time the fire of discord gets halfway to the top, the building can't be saved no matter how much water the fireman spray. That tipping point is called the point of no return.

So, how do people keep from reaching it? Lucky for me, I was offered the chance to learn from veteran couples. I was working for a newspaper when our marriage hit the hard times. My editor just happened to send me on a writing assignment that led me to an elderly couple. After 50 years together, they were still smitten. I remember thinking they must be newlyweds because of the way they treated each other. To my happy surprise, they were eager to share their wisdom. Visiting with silver haired duos still having fun gave me hope for the marriage I wanted. I wrote it years ago, but *Texas Twosomes Married for Life* still inspires me.

Every couple meets hurricane force winds at one time or another. The trick is to have enough good habits in place to brace up the marriage before the storm hits. What successful marriages seem to have in common is a desire to keep stoking the fire. Marriages set on cruise control will smash into a wall every time.

Making meals, riding bikes, taking walks, playing cards…these are good ways to keep the love light burning. Whatever the pastime, doing fun things together will keep spouses coming back for more. Everybody wants a good marriage, but not everybody wants to put the time in. Start with love, sprinkle in commitment and a pinch of luck, then stir in togetherness to your heart's content. Spending time together works every time.

# COMING FULL CIRCLE

Baby Boomers have seen it all.

People born between the year 1945 and 1965 have witnessed a myriad of changes. I was reminded of this fact yet again last night while getting ready for a date. My husband and I had reservations at a fancy downtown restaurant to celebrate the closing of a business deal. It was a special celebration, so I was taking my time to look my best. While applying the last strokes of mascara, I heard music.

With an upbeat, calliope-type melody, it sounded familiar. Still, I couldn't place it. I quickly painted my lips with my favorite lip gloss and traced the tune to its source. There in the front yard I found my husband, Jimmy. All dressed to go and leaning against a tree. He was watching children of all ages flock to the old fashioned ice cream truck. If we hadn't been on our way to a special night out, we probably would have bought a couple of Dreamsicles and hung out for awhile.

I texted my neighbor to make sure her kids didn't miss out on the fun. She wasn't nearly as excited as I was. "That guy has been rolling through the neighborhoods around here for awhile now," she said. It appears that those pied piper ice cream trucks are making a comeback. I'm glad. By the looks on the kids' faces, they are, too.

Watching kids lick ice cream on a stick triggered memories from my childhood. Suddenly, I saw ruddy faced Mr. Martin carting fresh eggs to our back door every Monday morning. To a family of 16, his delivery of 12 dozen was huge in more ways than one. Daddy scrambled a skillet full for breakfast every day. Something else I fondly recalled was the man from the cleaners who picked up our father's button down shirts on Tuesday afternoons. You think a lady with fourteen kids has time to iron?

With the turn of the 21$^{st}$ century, our society has gone from one end of the spectrum to the other. Full service has given way to plenty of self-serve and do-it-yourself projects. Our parents had their buttons pushed by official elevator operators in downtown department stores. Now Home Depot wants us to believe we can build our own.

American families have transitioned from eating pot roast in their dining rooms on Sundays to picking up fast food from nearby drive-throughs. These days, delivery means boxes of pizza or small white containers of sweet and sour pork. Wait. That's not true. People can order practically anything online. It will arrive within days on the front porch courtesy Fedex.

Life in general is getting faster and more expensive, but online deals await. Yesterday, I was complaining about how much I spent on my new glasses. My friend informed me of a cheap website for prescription lenses. Eighty percent cheaper? It sounds too good to be true.

But that's the Internet for you. It brings things to the front door just like the good old days. Would we ever go back? Trade the instant gratification of email for the anticipation of a letter from a loved one? Give up the convenience of facebook for cartons of eggs at the back door? Not a chance when grocery stores and farmer's markets are so close by. We can still get the feel of the fifties with trips to P. Terry's and Red Robin. Many cleaners still deliver. There are even stores that specialize in metal ice trays and pink foam rollers.

I suppose we have come full circle. Now we can live in whichever era we choose. It makes me smile to see a twenty-something female wearing a head full of hair rollers. My daughter's roommate curls her hair the old fashioned way, just like her mother and grandmother before her. Old or new? Fast or slow? Work the project myself or farm it out? At this point, everything is available. One simply needs to know where to look. Now if you'll excuse me, I think I hear the ice cream truck. That, my friend, is music to my ears.

# CONFESSIONS OF A PACKRAT IN RECOVERY

My husband and I share a bone of contention. He likes to throw thing things away and I like to keep them. He calls me a packrat, but that can't be right. A packrat keeps everything. I am extremely discerning. Some things are just too valuable to pitch out. Like that Kermit the frog costume I made for our son, Daniel, when he was a toddler. It was a Butterick pattern, for goodness sake. Do you know how hard it is to sew a Butterick pattern?

And then there was the rabbit hutch. When our second son, Will, was young he set his heart on adopting a bunny. His father and I promised that if he saved up half the money, we would spring for the rest. When I drove him to the breeder's house, he couldn't decide between the white one with pink ears or the furry brown one. By the time he made the choice, I loved Rascal as much as he did. On the way home, we bought a handmade hutch for the newest member of our family.

One morning a few months later, Will found Rascal on his back, paws up and glassy-eyed. Evidently, lop eared bunnies are not the sturdiest of the species. While Rascal wasn't with us long, his cage took up attic space for almost a decade. Every time my husband put it on the curb for the garbage men, I retrieved it. "We might get another rabbit", I argued. "It was an expensive cage", I said. I'm not really sure why I wanted to hold on to that thing. All I know is that every time I looked at it I remembered the megawatt smile on Will's 8 year old face the day we brought the bunny home.

I'm sentimental. Is that a good excuse for holding on to special things? "Your dad made that wooden duck on a string for the kids", I said when Jimmy tried to pitch it. "That toy truck was Daniel's favorite when he was 5 years old," I pleaded. It's a "push-pull" exercise for my husband and me. I simply can't part with meaningful momentos.

Truthfully, my problem goes beyond that. Yesterday I walked into our closet and noticed how packed it was. My hangers were so jammed, I couldn't see what was on them. My husband and I share a big closet. When we moved in, we divided the space judiciously. Over the years, my stuff has crept over the line.

Twenty shirts, twelve pairs of pants, a few blue jeans and three suits. That list just about sums up his wardrobe and he wears all of it regularly. I have shirts that I bought when the first George Bush was in office that I haven't worn since the second one left the White House. How many white blouses can one person wear, anyway?

As I perused all those outdated clothes, I was filled with a desire to purge. There is a Salvation Army store not far from my house. Lifting the hangers one at a time, I asked myself these questions: Do I ever wear it? Might someone else? Purging is easier when I tell myself that someone else may use it.

They say the first step to recovery is admitting there is a problem. My name is Donia and I am a packrat. When I was a teen, all the girls in the family shared a drawer for undergarments. Finding a bra that fit depended on how early you got up in the morning. No wonder it's hard to part with stuff. I asked a couple of my sisters if they were savers, too. "Absolutely!" they agreed. My oldest sister shared some encouragement. "The more you give away, the better you get at it."

She was right. In the middle of my closet cleanout, I felt a significant shift in attitude. By the end of it, I felt like a new woman. I still have packrat leanings, but now I'm in recovery. It feels great to let go, one white blouse at a time.

# COOKING UP A CHANGE

I came home from a dinner meeting last night to the aroma of fresh baked chocolate. If that's not the most intoxicating smell on the planet, I don't know what is. It was obvious that my husband had been busy in the kitchen. The brownies were still warm from the oven. Irresistible, one of them found its way to my mouth before I even put my purse down.

My husband bakes.

This is new territory. In the past, Jimmy has left the baking to me. Making goodies for friends and family is one of my favorite pastimes. A dozen banana muffins might welcome a neighbor to the neighborhood and applesauce cake is made for friends and family at Christmas time. Chocolate chip cookies can be found under the glass dome of the cake plate at least once a week. When the kids were little, I baked a cake every week.

My culinary creations are not anything special. In fact most of the credit goes to Duncan Hines and Betty Crocker. Thanks to Williams- Sonoma, I have an assortment of pans that add oomph to my baked goods. I put my stamp on them with shape and decoration. When our son Daniel turned 30, he got a cake in the shape of that number. A friend with a Valentine's Birthday has been graced with a heart shaped cake dripping in strawberry glaze. I get a serious kick out of producing sweets that please the eye and the palate. And now my husband is muscling in on my action?

The man has always known his way around the kitchen. That's part of what attracted me to him in the first place. On our third date, he invited me over for crayfish Etoufee. It was so full of cayenne, I couldn't eat more than one bite. That didn't matter. What he cooked was not as important as the effort he made in cooking it. Obviously, I was looking for a husband who knew what to do with a skillet. Daddy used to scramble eggs for the family every morning.

Jimmy does a lot of things well. After a few years of golf, he had whittled his handicap down to a five. He has only painted a few things in his life, but when he took a brush to our dining room cabinet, his strokes were smooth as silk. Do you see what I'm worried about? The guy is a quick study. There's every chance he could "best" me at baking.

Common sense tells me I should accept this new turn of events. Embrace it even. Now we have one more thing in common. When I think about it, the boundaries dividing our domestic duties have been blurring for years. I hang pictures. He does laundry. I mow the lawn. He does the dishes. It's possible that I may be overreacting here.

Most women would kill to have a husband like mine. In the past, when the girls came for dinner, he stayed in the bedroom buried in the baseball game. Last month, when they came, he served us wine. At the end of the evening when the weather turned nasty, he grabbed an umbrella. He walked each and every guest to her car in the pelting rain. They bragged about him for weeks afterward. My single friends still bring it up.

My husband has changed for the better. He is more far thoughtful than the man I married. Am I really going to whine when he bakes a few brownies? It sounds like I'm trying to have my cake and eat it too. A change of step has taken place in our domestic dance. Is it change for better or worse? If I'm in doubt about that, I should just ask my girlfriends. What difference does it make who bakes and who mows? Perhaps we should celebrate how far we've both come. On that sweet note, I'll have another brownie.

# COUNTING FAMILY BLESSINGS

Oranges can be surprisingly juicy during the winter time. While biting into a particularly good one this morning, I couldn't help thinking of my father in law, James. He grew up during The Great Depression. There were times when all Santa brought him and his four siblings was an orange in a stocking. One would think he'd never look at another one. That was not the case. He relished every bite of that sweet citrus fruit. Every time we came for a visit, he sliced the fruit to share with us. To him it was a delicacy.

There is another reason why I think of James Crouch at this time of year. Today is December 7th, the anniversary of Pearl Harbor. James played an important role during WWII. In fact, he was a war hero. Flying a B-17 bomber, he was shot down by the Germans. With shrapnel still embedded in his legs, he was taken to a prisoner of war camp where he spent 22 months.

He didn't speak about his war experiences to his sons when they were growing up. Fortunately, by the time I married his oldest boy, he was ready to chat. I'm grateful for those conversations over coffee and toast at the breakfast table. He shared even more details while addressing our son's fifth grade class. While we treasure that heartrending video, it's hard to watch him choke back tears. He told the story just like it happened.

He didn't complain about such things as starvation or solitary confinement. In fact, he appeared to take most of his prison camp life in stride. He spoke about the effects of hunger like a weatherman might report the Texas heat; as a matter of fact. The only thing that seemed to break his heart or his spirit was that so many of his friends didn't make it home.

In 1945, Patton's troops freed the camp survivors and James returned to his home town. That's when he met and married the love of his life. That's also when he built the house where his wife Reba still lives today. He built a successful life and a thriving business. Even his talent for selling insurance was eclipsed by his ability to fix things. In the twenty odd years I knew him, I never once heard of him calling a repair man. A hands-on homeowner, he taught his sons to be that way, too.

When we bought our first home, I saw few signs of those early lessons. However, the past few years have nudged my husband into projects that surprise me. Tasks like rebuilding a fence gate and installing a new garbage disposal no longer require a professional at our house. I'm so grateful that James defended our country, but I'm even more grateful for all the things he taught his son.

As I read my own words, it sounds like I'm recommending him for sainthood. Nothing could be further from the truth. His shortage of patience and impossibly high standards made him a sinner just like the rest of us. On the other hand, he worked hard for his family and never gave up no matter how difficult a situation became. I've been told that a saint is just someone who keeps trying to do the right thing.

Maybe that's why he and his peers are considered by many to be the greatest generation. Most veterans of WWII manifested "can do" spirits, unwavering work ethics and boat loads of integrity. If suffering builds character, it's easy to see why they had so much of it. They say the older we get, the more we become like our parents. As Jimmy racks up the miles on his odometer checking on his aging mother every month, I see a true reflection of his father's priorities. Obviously, he passed his values on to his son and I'm so glad he did. On Christmas morning, as we gather around the breakfast table, we will raise our orange juice glasses high. Here's to you, James Crouch. May your legacy live on in your children and grandchildren forever!

# COUSIN CANINES MEET AT LAST

We have three grown children. Only one of them still lives here in town. We don't get to see the out-of-town kids as often as we'd like. The only good thing about having family who live out of town is that when they come for a visit, they stay at the house with us. We get a highly concentrated visit. We like to stay up late watching movies. Then we lounge around the next morning drinking coffee and catching up on each other's lives.

When our son got married, his bride's 8 year old terrier was part of their wedding contract. So whenever the newlyweds come to visit, they bring their four-legged friend along. As his "grandparents", we have grown to love the little guy. When Caiden runs through our front door at Easter, Christmas, and Thanksgiving, we are happy to have him.

This year the plot thickened when our daughter adopted a dog. Now she brings her Heinz 57 pup whenever she comes to town, too. Like all puppies, 4 month old Piper is bursting with energy and enthusiasm. Her legs are already long enough to get her into trouble. Caiden is short, squatty and seasoned with age. They are different in every way. We have been around each of them quite a few times but the two of them have never met. We couldn't help wondering how they would get along when they found themselves under the same roof. Ours.

So here is a description of the scene that followed our daughter and her dog's arrival at midnight after a very long car ride. The long legged boxer mix stood staring at the pint sized terrier in our foyer.

"Say hello to your cousin, Caiden". Daniel nudged the little guy toward his fellow canine. Caiden looked at the dog, then up at Daniel, and then back at the dog. Next he did that tilted head thing that dogs do when they are confused. The look on his face said: "There must be some mistake. She could not possibly be my cousin! Look at those ears!" At that point, his ears went straight up, his tail was like a rod and he slowly started backing away.

Piper was undaunted. Three times his size, she lunged and nipped at the older dog. "Come on, let's play, let's play, let's play!" she seemed to say. With every backward step of Caidens came more unbridled enthusiasm from the pup. Caiden was desperate. His eyes pleaded with Daniel. "Have you gone mad?" he said with a growl. "I have been an only child for 8 years. I've never even spent an afternoon with another dog, much less a punk without manners."

He had a point. Suddenly, both dogs began barking loud enough to wake the dead. All the humans stood in a semi circle watching and waiting for signs of acceptance. We tried to convince each other they would soon be fast friends. Given the unrelenting barking, it was not an easy sell.

The next day brought more of the same. It was a hectic and not very relaxing Saturday. Finally, by Sunday afternoon, the young pup had actually learned a few things. Most important of all, she had learned what parts of Caiden's anatomy were off limits for sniffing. I am happy to report that both dogs survived the "cousin canines encounter".

There was no bloodshed to speak of. On the other hand, they won't be sharing "Beggin' Strips" any time soon. We decided it might be smart to keep them apart until Piper gets a little bit older. Still, they both took home a valuable lesson. Piper has learned that her nose is not welcome in certain places. Caiden has learned that family is family, even if the new cousin has weird ears.

# DOGS AND BABIES
# BRING OUT SOFT SIDE

When I woke up yesterday, my husband's side of the bed was empty. Exhausted from driving our way through the holidays, I had slept in. So did our daughter who had come to visit for a few days. Jimmy was the only one awake. Then who the heck was my hubby talking to in the living room? And why did his voice sound so funny?

Oh yeah. He was talking to his "grand dog" in that strange baby language he reserves just for her. It makes me smile to watch him with our daughter's dog because he shows a side of himself I've never seen. "Good dog, Piper, good dog" are the words he spoke. But they came out more like "Goooooooooood dooooooooooooog Piiiiiiper, goooooooooooooood dooooooog".

Add a backwards baseball cap, sunglasses, and finger snapping and we might have a decent rap song. After crooning, he rubbed her belly and then treated her to a whole bunch of ear scratching. When Piper noticed me sitting all by myself on the couch with nothing but coffee and newspaper for company, she trotted over to rest her head on my thigh. After a minute or two, he called her back over. I think he was jealous.

He wasn't anything like this with our own dogs. We raised three along with our kids. While there was no doubt about Jimmy's love for Charcoal, Sugar and Spice, his displays of affection for them were considerably more reserved. He patted their heads when he came home from work. He threw tennis balls for them to fetch whenever he was with them in the backyard, but he never treated them like babies. And he never lit up like a Christmas tree when they came through the door.

My neighbor says her middle aged husband treated their dog like a person, too. He saved a spot on the couch just for Lillie, their miniature schnauzer. He fed her directly from his plate at the dinner table and let her sleep at the foot of their bed every night. His wife begged him to stop spoiling her. "She's a dog," she reminded him. With every reminder, he nodded agreeably and continued to do the same thing.

Mike and Sherry have 2 dachschunds. The other evening, Sherry and I joined friends for a "Girl's Night Out". When I pulled up in front of her house, Mike walked her to the car. I asked him about his plans for the evening and he broke into a big grin. "I'm picking Duchess and Daisy up from the groomer in a little while. We're going to watch the football game together".

My sister's husband, who raised three daughters with a very firm hand, became an absolute marshmallow when Muffie, the cocker spaniel, took up residence. When their granddaughters were born, he poured on even more attention than he had given the dog. Is that how it works? Men mellow with age? They treat grandbabies and grand dogs with progressively more tender loving care and coddling?

Many friends have traveled the road to grandparenthood ahead of us. It seems like women always go "gaga" over grandchildren but with men, it's not a given. Some get directly in touch with their soft side. Others manifest a more reserved style. It appears that the ones who treat their dogs like babies are the ones who treat their grandkids like treasures. Will Jimmy be the type of grandfather who rolls around on the floor with our little ones? Our daughter-in-law is pregnant, so we are about to find out. This time next year, the lad will be 6 months old.

Now it's Sunday afternoon. Our daughter packed up our "grand dog" and headed home hours ago. Hubby and I stood on the curb and watched her SUV get smaller. Now that she lives closer, she comes to see us more often, but it's still hard to watch her drive away. It's even harder now with Piper in the picture. "Did she mention when they might be back?" Jimmy asked as we walked into the house. Which type of grandfather will Jimmy be? That's a rhetorical question.

# EVERY BLESSING COUNTS

Some people call me Pollyanna. I've been accused of putting a positive and sometimes unrealistic spin on whatever happens. Perhaps that's true. I admit to believing that if I think about something long enough, I will surely find something good about it. One thing is for sure. If wrote down all the blessings and curses of my entire life, the list of happy occurrences would be significantly longer than the list of unfortunate ones. Maybe I should write down both for a while, just to prove my point.

It seems an especially good time for an experiment of the sort because our family has recently received devastating news. Our daughter's fiancé is seriously ill. Upon hearing the diagnosis, I searched for my Pollyanna persona. She was nowhere to be found. Instead of upbeat and positive, I felt angry and anxious. God and I had a heated discussion. "My words were loud and bitter." "Haven't we had enough hurt for awhile?" "Surely, our hardship quota has been met". Hardships are tests of faith. Haven't we passed enough tests?"

The day after our world got rocked, I was still mad. I vented to a friend at church. When she saw how spiritually bankrupt and ungrateful I was, her eyes lit up. "I have just the thing." With that, she reached into the back of her car and pulled out a copy of the New York Times bestseller, *One Thousand Gifts* by Ann

Voskamp. She said she had already read it twice. She was convinced it would help.

Voskamp is a farmer's wife and a homeschooling mother of six. She "dared herself to live fully right where she was" when she wrote the book that changed her life. It all started when a friend challenged her to count her gifts until they totaled one thousand. Blessings journals are nothing new, but aren't they usually reserved for keeping track of the good stuff? Voskamp offered a completely different perspective on gratitude. *Morning shadows across old floors? Jam piled high on toast?* As you can see, the blessings she records are in no way remarkable.

After years of limping along with a broken heart, she felt healed by simple images of everyday life. In this painfully real piece of non-fiction, she says blessings are sometimes hidden inside hellish experiences. For her, that discovery led to a softening of the heart. For her, it initiated much needed healing.

Sitting beside our son-in-law's bed in the hospital room this past weekend, I had plenty of time to ponder her practice. Instead of "*Why us?*" a different question sprang to my mind. Would my faith still carry me through if I didn't embrace the struggle? My path to joy might be waiting just beyond the intersection of acceptance and faith.

Did you know that it's physically impossible to be grateful and angry at the same time? That's radical gratitude for you. On the way to the medical center parking garage, I realized that I'm the only one who can change my attitude. Will I walk down the ramp of thankfulness or bitterness?

Just a few days ago, I was in the middle of a full blown pity party. And then an inspired friend handed me her new favorite book. Now I'm too busy saying thank you God on my own journal pages to feel sorry for my family or myself. I found beauty in these blessings.

*Driving for miles to pray over new brother*
*Laying on of healing hands*
*Dedicated doctors consulting at midnight*

Faced with discouraging MRIs and dropping platelet counts, we are still praying for a miracle. Taylor says "God has a plan". Does this plan involve spiritual, emotional or physical healing? At this point, we don't know. We will continue to look for blessings every step along the way.

# FAMILY MEMORIES FLOOD THE CAMP

Cockle doodle doo! That was the sound of my wake-up call this morning. No need for an alarm clock when an able bodied rooster lives down the road. We are out in the country this weekend. I am sitting on a porch swing with my mother-in-law watching birds peck the lawn for breakfast. If you are looking for relief from the pressure of city life, the woods of East Texas have a lot to offer. My late father-in-law knew that better than anyone. He bought this lake property back in the sixties.

I heard about "The Camp" long before I married into the family. Jimmy started talking about it on our first date. He and his brothers helped their dad build it while they were still in high school. Plumbers and electricians were hired for the technical jobs, but the hammer and saw part was saved for the Crouch boys.

As soon as the house was completed, Jimmy started bringing his buddies for duck hunts and fishing trips. I didn't get to be a regular until after we married and had kids. I quickly discovered that, for the kids, a weekend in the country with Mamaw and Papaw was almost as exciting as Christmas morning. For Daniel's 4th birthday, we bought a pint sized 4-wheeler. That kicked the fun quotient into overdrive.

Then Papaw purchased a small metal trailer to hook on the back of his riding lawnmower. That way he and his granddaughter could ride along beside Daniel and Will. Reba and I watched from our lawn chairs as the happy parade kicked up dust on the road in front of the house. We held our breaths and said a prayer whenever our youngest was along for the ride. Miracle of miracles, she never fell out of her carpet covered carriage.

Everything felt like an adventure at The Camp. Even manual labor was enticing. Daniel found that out when he painted the porch. His paint job has lasted two decades. "He was only sixteen when he did that!" Reba was delighted that her grandkids had an interest in the place. "Did Donia Cain hang that shelf," she asked.

Maybe that's why we love it here. We've all invested a bit of sweat equity. I like to burn branches and mow the lawn. Our daughter has added lamps and rearranged the furniture. Like his father before him, Jimmy is a fixer. Today he installed screen panels on the back porch. The clerks at Big Tin Barn call him by name.

We bring different things to the Camp but everybody leaves with memories. Reba takes home more than anyone. She's traveled far and wide. Her eyes light up when she reminisces about watching the leaves change in Vermont or taking in the water lilies of Monet's Paris Gardens, but her most treasured times happened with her grandkids in the Piney woods of East Texas. She adores this place so don't offer to take her there unless you really mean it. She will grab her walker and be waiting in the front seat before you can say Lake Sam Rayburn.

Now it's Sunday and it's time to go home, but we're treating ourselves to one more "go" on the porch swing.

There is nothing like watching the rain fall softly on the Pine trees. As the raindrops fall harder, the bark of the trees gets darker. I notice a puddle that's starting to collect on the floor of the screened in porch. Even raindrops falling on our heads can't dampen our matriarch's outlook. "I believe that's the first leak we've ever had in this house," she says brightly. "Jimmy will take care of it."

Whether we're fixing things, having fun or just hanging out, we make new memories with every trip. Papaw knew what he was doing when he bought this lot in the woods for his family. Taking care of The Camp is another way of taking care of each other. Memories are made of this.

# A SECOND CHANCE AT LIFE AND LOVE

S econd chances aren't as rare as one might think. People get them every day. They come in different forms, too. Some folks get a second chance at life while others get another crack at love.

My brother in law knows what I'm talking about. He used to make a living by delivering automotive supplies. His daily route spanned 180 miles each way. One day, halfway finished with his commute, he passed out behind the wheel of his truck. Amazingly, he didn't injure himself or anyone else after losing consciousness on the highway. He opened his eyes to a half dozen strangers surrounding his truck. They were banging on the windows and yelling, "Are you okay?" One of them called 911. The paramedics were on the scene ASAP. He had suffered a heart attack.

After being shocked back to life in an ambulance, he was delivered to a nearby hospital where the doctors assessed his coronary needs. The day after the accident, I went to visit him. He shared the dramatic story, at least all that he could remember, of his "close call". "The doctors believe I was extremely lucky", he said. "Maybe I should buy a lottery ticket."

We laughed at his joke, but there was nothing funny about his scrape with death. He was lucky in two ways: no one was injured when he crashed and he suffered no permanent brain damage from the lack of blood flow from his heart. Thank God for cell phones and record response time by the emergency medical technicians.

It happened on a Tuesday. An overloaded surgery schedule in a busy hospital forced him to be patient. He waited three days for his turn in the operating room. Throughout that time, his intake was restricted. Liquid diet, but plenty of food for thought. His older brother died at the age of 67 from heart disease. My infirmed in-law was following in his deceased sibling's footsteps. Seventy five pounds overweight with high blood pressure and diabetes, he received specific post op instructions. "Lose weight and exercise."

It's hard for most people to maintain exercising programs. It's tougher for him because, thanks to four years on the high school football team, his knees don't have any cartilage to speak of. Just walking to the kitchen is difficult for him. Finding ways to burn calories will be a major challenge. From where I'm sitting, it looks as if he has no choice.

Stuck in an Intensive Care Unit waiting for life-saving surgery? It's a blinking red caution light if ever I've seen one. Passing the rooms of seriously ill people on my way to visit him, I wondered how many of his fellow patients would make it out of there alive. My brother-in-law's story had a happy ending. His heart surgery went well. A week later, he was issued his discharge papers; a second chance at life.

Some get a second chance at love. Like the couple whose wedding we danced at last night. They have both been married before. Standing on a hill in front of 100 friends and family, they pledged their vows with the evening sun warming all of our faces. His three young children stood beside them -dressed up and smiling. They welcomed their new stepmom with enthusiasm. That's something to be thankful for all by itself. The rehearsal dinner was joyful- loved ones passed the mic one to another offering heart-felt toasts. The groom's teen-aged nephew made us laugh with his advice: "Make this one last!" I think they will. They seem to know how lucky they are.

As does my brother-in-law with the repaired heart. Upon leaving the hospital, he beamed like a man who had won the lottery. No more chicken fried steak for him. He also talked of starting some kind of exercise routine. He probably would have promised the moon if that's what it took to get him out of the hospital. "I really hope you'll do those things," I said, hugging him goodbye. "You're lucky to get a second chance."

As I turned to walk away, he called out in his booming voice, "So do you!" I gave him a puzzled look. "Everybody gets one," he explained. "It's called tomorrow."

# FEAR OF FAMILY FEEDBACK

I t's time to get back on my wheels.

A few months ago, I broke my collarbone. The very next day an orthopedic surgeon reassembled me with a titanium plate and nine lovely screws. Ten days later, the stitches were healed. A month after that, I returned for my post-op appointment and was pronounced good to go. Unlike Humpty Dumpty, I had been put back together again. As I picked up my things to leave the examination room, my trusty doctor cleared me for whatever activity I felt like doing.

I stopped dead in my tracks. "Anything?" I asked him. "You mean I can ride my bike again?" With a confident smile, he tapped my collarbone. "You couldn't re-injure that bone if you tried," he said referring to the heavy duty hardware he had installed in my clavicle. All the way home, I thought about pumping up my tires, jumping on the bike and riding down the street with the wind in my hair.

That was weeks ago and I still haven't put my hands on the handlebars. Until now, I couldn't admit the real reason why not. Or maybe I'm just now figuring it out. I'm afraid, that's why I haven't mounted my bicycle. I'm chock full of old fashioned, unadulterated fear. But it's not fear of breaking another bone. It's not even fear of falling. It's fear of family feedback.

For years, I have been riding my bike places my husband and children don't want me to go. It all started when we lived in a subdivision right off a major highway. I got up at sunrise and rode my bike all the way to the elementary school where I taught. Nine miles and forty five minutes later, I pulled into the parking lot feeling as if I had scaled Mount Everest. The endorphin rushes that followed those trips were more powerful than any high I have ever felt from alcohol. They lasted twice as long, too. *I Am Woman, Hear Me Roar* I thought, as I made my way through the building to the ladies locker room.

In those days, I also counted on pedal power to get me to my neighborhood library. Any errands accomplished on a bike made me feel strong and independent. It was good to know that if I had to, I could get along without car insurance or gasoline.

Don't get me wrong. Not all bike rides have led me to a blissful state. Even without crashing, I have found myself in the position of needing roadside assistance. Last May while pedaling home in hundred degree heat, I finally gave up and called our son, Will. That cell phone SOS was a tough one to send. Our middle child had warned me that very morning of the unseasonably hot weather predicted in the forecast. To his credit, he never spoke one word of reproach. He just pulled up beside me and loaded me and the bike into his car. No doubt, the words were on his mind, but he never said, "I told you so" aloud.

For that matter, nobody in the family has ever uttered that phrase. But that was before "the fall". That was before they watched me undergo the pain and suffering of a fractured collarbone, an allergic reaction to the anesthetic, an emergency trip to the opthomalogist, (don't ask) and, due to lousy insurance, an excruciating hit to our pocketbook.

Staring at my ten-speed bike, I asked myself a question. What's the worst that could happen if I fell again? Instead of obsessing over family judgment, maybe I could do a few things to minimize that possibility. I could ride slower, stay on the sidewalk, keep my eyes on the path in front of me and shorten my trips.

That settles it. There is absolutely no reason to be afraid of falling. I will trust myself and my family to do the right thing. Why am I worrying about what my tribe thinks, anyway? I am the one who decides when and where I should ride. Suddenly, it's a beautiful day for a spin around the block.

# FINDING A WAY TO LET GO

Our son in law, Taylor, died last Friday. In spite of his steady decline, we were caught off guard by his death at the age of 29. By the time he was diagnosed, the cancer had already metastasized. Still, he managed to live longer than any of the doctors thought he would. A fighter till the end, he packed a lot of life into those last 87 days. Our daughter, his wife for 40 of them, will never forget him. None of us will.

Some people collect friends wherever they go… school, church, football games, work, even a hospital. That was Taylor. With his can-do spirit and infectious smile, he won everyone over. I'm thinking of one member of his support team who took a particular shine to Taylor. Toward the end of his life, she cried every time she left his bedside. His passing provoked a lot of tears.

But not everyone shows grief by crying. We learned that from the oncology counselor who was there for us whenever we needed her. People move through loss differently she said. There is no right or wrong way to grieve. Some talk their way through it- sharing stories and memories with loved ones. Some go into a closet and sob all by themselves. As many personalities as there are on this earth, that's how many different ways there are to get through.

The important thing is to get what we need. Wearing a smile for the sake of others is a bad idea. If I feel depressed, I give myself permission to burrow into bed and pull the covers over my head. On the other hand, stuffing my feelings will never help. Pretending happiness will only slow down the healing process and hurt in the long run.

Yesterday I walked around our back yard to find that recent rains had peppered the flower beds with weeds. Yard work has always been therapeutic for me, so I sat down on a big, flat rock and started pulling those bad boys out by the fistful. Our yard backs up to an oak-filled greenbelt which offers privacy as well as inspiration. As lovely as it was to be surrounded by God's beauty, I was soon bawling like a baby.

Afterwards, when I walked back into the house and looked at the kitchen clock, I realized that my floodgates had opened at exactly the same time Taylor died seven days before. I hadn't anticipated a biological reaction, but when I stopped to think, it made perfect sense. The heart knows what to do before the brain even engages. Tears are a healing salve for many folks. I'm one of them.

My husband is not. While Jimmy is more in touch with his feelings now than he has ever been, his emotions are still quite a bit more buttoned up than mine. Happy or sad, I let my feelings flow. I don't care where I am or who is watching. Even if it makes those around me uncomfortable, which it sometimes does, I believe in crying.

When I came in from the garden yesterday, my husband was standing in the kitchen. When he saw my puffy eyes, he opened his arms and I walked right into them. I used to hide those "ugly cries" from him because I knew they made him feel uncomfortable. As we have grown together, my need to be honest trumps his need for control. "Let it all out," he said. So I did.

Many years ago, a friend's 8-year-old daughter suddenly dropped dead of an undiagnosed heart defect. The little girl collapsed in the middle of her own birthday party. That was 18 years ago. I still remember the primal sound of her mother's sobs. When I run into Linda at the grocery store, we might even talk about her daughter. Sometimes we shed a tear together. It feels really good to remember.

Anyone who hides feelings for fear of looking fragile might want to re-think that plan. There is nothing strong about it. Find a nook or a friend and wail away. Or not. There is a different path for everyone. The challenge lies in finding one's way.

# FLU BONDS LIKE SUPER GLUE

Our bed stayed unmade for ten days. That's because there was always at least one of us in it. For the better part of two weeks, my husband and I remained horizontal. An angry germ with our name on it settled over us with a vengeance. We took Tamiflu and Emergen-C. We guzzled orange juice by the gallon, but it didn't seem to help. This was the year a big, bad bug had come to stay.

It was also the year we decided not to get flu shots. I'm not sure why. Did we think we were immune? I did. After many years of avoiding the "epizootus" (that's what Uncle Tommy used to call it), I felt invincible. Even after friends and family began dropping like flies around me. My sister, Judi and her spouse caught a mean strain. She informed me, long distance in between bouts of coughing that the flu had become an epidemic in Atlanta. Her husband stayed home from work for 5 days. That was something he had not done in thirty years. Then he got well and she got sick, dropping 6 pounds in the process. She did not have the extra weight to lose.

I felt sorry for them. Yes, but my compassion was tainted with cockiness. So blessed with great health for so long, I took it for granted. Even when teaching a classroom of kids with runny noses, I had managed to escape the worst of it. Note to self: Smug feelings will come back to haunt you. I felt feverish just hours after hanging up the phone with my sister. It was as if the germs had traveled through the phone line. My temperature suddenly soared to 102 degrees. I went through boxes of tissues and throat lozenges faster than my husband could buy them.

Not used to seeing me that way, Hubby rose to the occasion. He has an office in our house, so he took care of me along with his real estate business. Make a phone call, check on the wife. Take a meeting, check on the wife. Bowls of chicken soup and glasses of juice appeared on a wooden tray beside me. Whatever I asked for, he delivered.

Sick as I was, I couldn't help but feel grateful. I knew how good I had it. My husband was helping me get better. But then he caught the bug. We were in the bed together, sneezing and coughing. Conversation was limited to "Pass the thermometer" and "Are we out of Kleenex?!" We were cranky and germy and totally bummed.

Over the years, we have split a lot of things, but this was our first time to share an infection. His and her towels are nice, his and her razors essential, but his and her flu? Was it my imagination or were we, in the middle of our infirmities, competing to see whose symptoms were worse?

Thankfully, my flu ran its course before his did. I knew I wouldn't die of it, but that didn't keep me from wanting to. My first day back in the world was exciting. I walked through Wal Mart swinging a giant jug of orange juice. I smiled at other customers and felt an actual spring in my step. *I remember what this is,* I said to myself. *It's energy.*

Walking back into the house, I unloaded the bag of goods. "Another cup of hot tea?" I called from the kitchen. I couldn't wait to nurture my spouse. "Do you need more aspirin?" I asked. It's easy to wait on loved ones when you feel good yourself. The flu brings out the worst in the patient, but the best in the caregiver.

It's no fun to be sick, but taking care does wonders for relationships. When you have your health, you have everything. When you have a spouse willing and able to nurse you through maladies, that is even better. Who knew? Flu bonds couples like super glue.

I'm grateful to get this winter behind us. As unpleasant as our "down time" was, it inspired an idea for something else we can do together. It's a twist on date night: His and Her flu shots, and then dinner and a movie.

# FOR BETTER OR WORSE?

It was Sunday afternoon of Thanksgiving weekend. My daughter and her fiancé had packed up for their trip back home. As they rolled down the driveway, my husband suggested that we get the boxes from the attic and start decorating for Christmas. Since you don't know my husband, this probably sounds plausible. Lots of folks replace their scarecrows, pumpkins and hay bales with Santa Clauses before the turkey day tryptophan is out of their bloodstreams.

However, my hubby has never been one of those people. I learned a long time ago that he doesn't like to be rushed. He likes to get one holiday completely behind him before heading down the road to the next one. A weekend filled with family, too much cooking, overeating and nonstop football is enough without adding the labor intensive transition into Santa's big scene.

And yet here he was, dragging boxes and hanging garland like an elf possessed. Last year, I had to beg him for help. This year, he was leading the effort. As surprised as I was to witness this new attitude, I tried to act blasé about it. No sense in endangering his newfound enthusiasm. I watched silently as he stood at the top of a rickety ladder. He leaned against the roof with a string of lights in one hand and an extension cord in the other. "What do you think?" he called out as he snapped frosted white bulbs into their plastic holders.

What I think is that aliens have taken my husband away and left me with his look-alike. Of course, I didn't say that out loud. I was determined not to rock his holiday boat. At that point he had unpacked every strand of outdoor lighting we'd purchased over the past 3 decades and was energetically draping the front yard with them. There was one more surprise. He didn't seem to have a plan.

This guy who carefully researches and double checks everything was hanging over the roof on a ladder older than he, deciding as he went along where to hang the next section. In the past he would have drawn the design on paper, counted the plugs, and measured the strings. He would have made at least 3 trips to Home Depot. The end result would have screamed symmetry and conventionality.

I watched my husband fly by the seat of his pants for the first time in our married life. I will take this over any scene Hallmark ever came up with. After descending the ladder, he stood in front of the house admiring his handiwork. It was an odd assortment of white lights and colored ones. The strings hung loosely and without a pattern.

"I like it," he said.

"I like it too," I replied but I wasn't talking about the Christmas decorations. What thrilled my soul was his new and improved "laid back" attitude. When we got married in June of 1977, it didn't escape my mother's notice that I was committing myself to life with my polar opposite. My spouse is organized. He keeps pristine records of everything we do or buy and adheres to schedules as if his life depends on it. I like to play things by ear. I change my mind often. He worries. I laugh. He buys insurance. I take risks. Recently, Momma pointed out something I had yet to realize. "He is becoming more like you", she said. "I was hoping it would go the other way."

I laughed because I had hoped the same thing. We had both presumed that over time his planning and organizational skills would rub off on me. If we are each other's better half, then a good marriage will prompt changes that improve both of us. Right?

Perhaps it's time for me to take a personal inventory. Have I adopted any positive habits or characteristics? Surely, I have. Who is to say what is positive and negative, anyway? Maybe a better question is this. Has marriage changed us for better or worse? Perhaps I'll plug in those Christmas lights and think about it.

# FRIEND IN NEED IS BEST KIND

" Neither a borrower nor a lender be".

I don't know where Shakespeare got the idea that borrowing was a bad thing. Maybe he had a deadbeat brother. In my world, both borrowing and lending have proven themselves invaluable. My current neighbor and I frequently knock on each other's door for an egg or a cup of sugar. During the Christmas holidays, we borrowed everything from nutmeg to coffee. I'm pretty sure that Gina enjoys the convenience of borrowing as much as I do.

We're both from big families. Maybe that has something to do with it. When you grow up in a crowd, you learn the dance of give and take early. Three of my sisters and I were close in age and size, so we loaned each other clothes, shoes, money...even on the rare occasion, boyfriends. Not sharing was simply not an option at our house.

There was a time when I actually preferred my sisters' wardrobes to my own. When Cindy was 18, I was 17, Carol was 16 and Judy was 15, we babysat every week for spending money. My earnings were usually spent on consumables like candy and magazines. My siblings spent their money in more fashionable ways. Mary and Carol often made their way to Battlestein's, an upscale department store just down the street. They might come home with a paisley minidress or a pair of leather flats. Remember Papagallos? Those buttery soft leather shoes that came in every color of the rainbow back in the sixties? I couldn't bring myself to pay the high price of that trendy footware, but once they were sitting in my sister's closet, I couldn't resist slipping into them. I really couldn't help myself. Borrowing was in my blood.

After we got married, my biological clock ticked faster than my husbands. He suggested that I borrow my older sister's toddler. It was a good way to manage my maternal urge. I figured that when I had children, my younger sisters would take their turns "borrowing" from me. Unfortunately, by the time our kids came along, we had moved to another city. It was disappointing not to be in a position to share a babysitting coop with my sisters. I tried to get something going with the young moms in my new neighborhood.

It didn't take. Other mothers were more than willing to watch my rowdy offspring when I needed a haircut or a visit to the doctor. However, they never let me look after theirs. What kind of a relationship is that? A few years later, we moved again to a neighborhood with a larger pool of stay-at-home moms. This time, I struck it rich. My next door neighbor understood the fine art of reciprocity.

We have lived in 6 different houses over the course of our marriage, so I have had plenty of opportunities to train new members. Our children learned the borrowing system by osmosis. At one point our 6 year old tried to practice the concept. The results were embarrassing. Daniel was invited to a friend's house for lunch. While the babysitter was preparing peanut butter sandwiches, he convinced his friend that hot dogs would be better. They went next door and asked the neighbor if she could spare a couple of frankfurters. Our son was not invited back.

It was awkward when his buddy's mom brought him home early, but I couldn't blame our child. I had failed to convey an important principle. Borrowing is reserved for needed items like a cup of milk for cornbread when one's dinner guests are on their way. Or a ride to the repair shop when one's auto is ready and a spouse is out of town.

After two years, my current neighbor and I have taken the practice to a new level. We borrow each others' opinions and lend "shoulders to cry on" more than anything else. Allowing ourselves to become friends in need has bonded us in a beautiful way. There is nothing as rewarding as sharing one's heart.

# GATHERING FRIENDS
# AROUND KITCHEN TABLE

My parents entertained often while I was growing up. Making people feel welcome was one of Momma's special talents. She also had a knack for making them smile. Parading her 14 kids through the living room usually did that. It also did a lot to enhance Daddy's oil pipe sales. We couldn't sing like the children in *The Sound of Music,* but we knew how to work a crowd. The teenagers delivered cocktails. The toddlers charmed even the most cynical clients by bouncing through the dining room in their flannel pajamas.

Since cooking was not her forte, Momma became proficient at passing prepared food off as her own. An entrée that was sure to impress came from a seafood restaurant in Lafayette. That yummy roux, full of shrimp and okra, arrived in Houston on the day of her dinner parties via Greyhound bus. It was Daddy's job to pick it up from the downtown terminal. Then Momma transferred it to a cast iron pot on the back of the stove. The savory bouquet filled the house just in time for the arrival of their first guest. Ladled into china bowls, it always earned rave reviews. Momma graciously accepted all compliments. After all, she was the one who ordered it.

In our early years of marriage, my husband and I threw parties, too. In fact, I tossed him a birthday party the first 7 years of our marriage. Not to be outdone by my mother, I cooked gumbo and rented tables and chairs to accommodate our guests. During the eighties when we had more money than sense, we hired someone to help serve and clean. That kind of indulgence has not been repeated since.

When our kids hit the teen years, our social life began to change. It was dictated by the sports they played. We hung out with their team members' parents. Our gatherings happened quite naturally after games at the closest Mexican restaurant. They were "no mess, no fuss" dinners. As hectic as life with high schoolers is, that was about all we could manage.

Before we knew it, we were empty nesters. By then, we had the time and resources to entertain again, but had cultivated the habit of dining out. That was a hard habit to break. Whenever I tried to have a group over for dinner, the first invitee always talked me out of it. "Why go to all that trouble at home," said my girlfriend, "when we could meet somewhere and let the restaurant staff do the work?"

It was a convincing argument, but I knew in my heart that "all that trouble" would be worth it. Last week, I took the plunge and invited the bible study group over. With their prayers and moral support, these ladies had carried us through the difficult months of our son-in-law's cancer journey. I wanted to thank them. I wanted to meet their husbands.

So Jimmy threw some fish on the grill and I put a cake in the oven. Our guests brought everything else which really cut down on the workload. I couldn't help but think, as I was hanging clean towels in the powder room, about the first time we entertained. We were still newlyweds. Young and foolish, I vacuumed and scrubbed the apartment for days beforehand.

How silly I was back then. I actually thought people cared about such things. My older and wiser sister tried to tell me: Don't clean anything that someone riding through your house on a fast horse would not notice. I didn't listen then, but now I firmly adhere to that philosophy.

Friends don't come for fancy food or impressive housekeeping. They just want to feel at home. Breaking bread with friends around the kitchen table bonds people like nothing else. If the quality of our recent party can be measured by the laughter shared over chocolate cake, we scored a hit.

We took turns telling tales of courtships. Even the guys enjoyed hearing sweetheart stories. One couple took us back to their college days. She chased him until he caught her, she told us in between bites of dessert. While clearing the table and loading the dishwasher, we discussed dates for our next gathering. With a bit of effort, we could keep this practice going. The only question is this: Will we sit around the table at your house or mine?

# GOD WORKS HIS TIMELINE

When my husband and I got married 34 years ago, our union was known as a mixed marriage. I was Catholic and he was Baptist. I made a point to let him know exactly how Catholic I was all through our courtship. It sounds inflexible, but I wanted to make sure he knew that I was not available for a change of faith. Not a problem, he said. He wasn't attached to the Baptist church anyway.

My mother was a cradle Catholic, my father was a cradle Catholic. Together they produced 14 cradle Catholics. I was 6th from the top. I have always treasured my faith. Jimmy knew exactly what he was getting into. To seal the deal, on our wedding day, the priest handed him a paper to sign. It was a commitment to raise our children Catholic. Some of my sisters married non Catholics who balked at this. To my great relief, Jimmy didn't hesitate to sign on the dotted line.

So far, so good. He had agreed to get married in a Catholic church by a Catholic priest and baptize all future children Catholic. He showed no interest in becoming a Catholic himself. For some reason, I wasn't concerned. I figured it would either happen or it wouldn't. During our first years of marriage, we fell into a routine. Sunday morning meant Mass for me and sports on TV for him. That might have lasted forever if it hadn't been for the kids.

One day our four year old asked him a pointed question: "Why do I have to go to church if you don't?"

Daddy had no answer, so he got dressed and went with us. A few years later, Jimmy's younger brother married a Catholic woman and converted to Catholicism without delay. I wondered if his brother might inspire him to take the plunge? No, but he did continue attending Mass every Sunday. We held hands every Sunday morning and prayed with our church community: Our Father who art in Heaven hallowed be thy name...

Married life was blissful at first. Sometime during our second decade, things became quite difficult. Money problems, teenagers, anger issues... the conflicts seemed endless. We met with a marriage counselor off and on. We tried our best to honor date night but life was busy and complicated. The one thing we stayed faithful to was Sunday Mass. No matter what happened over the weekend, we went to church. Every Sunday we joined hands and prayed: Forgive us our sins as we forgive those...

After 22 years, he surprised me. "I wouldn't mind being in a bible study," he said, "if Father Jordan would lead it." Next thing we knew, and it seemed like a miracle at the time, our busy pastor and 8 neighbors were gathering in our home the first Wednesday evening of every month. When that study ended, we signed up for another one. This time we met in the choir room at church. He was the only non-Catholic in that group.

I remember thinking he sure had gotten a lot of nudges toward Catholicism over the years. Ironically, they seem to come from everyone but me. The Holy Spirit was working overtime. The less I pushed, the more I got what I had dreamed of: sharing my faith with my husband.

One day, we ran into the priest who had baptized our daughter more than 20 years earlier. After visiting with Father Scott at a mutual friend's house, Jimmy was excited to reconnect with him. "We should invite him to dinner," he said. So we did.

We weren't even halfway through the chicken and rice casserole when Father leaned over and asked an awkward question, "How come you never became a Catholic?" Shocked at his candor, I held my breath. My husband doesn't like being grilled, especially in front of others. His response was another surprise. "Honestly, Father, I don't know".

The next time Father came for dinner, he brought along some reading material. "These are for you," he said to Jimmy. The process was low key but highly effective . They met once a week to discuss the basic tenets of the faith. A few months later, in a private ceremony, Jimmy received his confirmation.

That's the story of how, after 33 years, my husband joined my faith. Without any pressure from me, my mother, my father or any of my 14 brothers and sisters, he said yes to an elderly priest he hadn't seen in 15 years. God works in mysterious ways. More importantly, He works his timeline, not ours.

# GOING TO THE DOGS

The human population may be dwindling in this country, but the number of dogs is growing every day. An industry that supports that growth is also exploding. Dog groomers, doggy daycare and hotels that say "Come!" are popping up on every corner. There are bakeries that produce nothing but canine treats and stores that specialize in pet clothing. Petsmart alone has 438 items to help Fido feel fashionable. On my visit to their website, I found hoodies in the hottest colors, leg warmers, 4 to a set, and a halter style terry cloth doggy dress that left me shaking my head.

Last month, our newspaper ran a feature story about the latest trends regarding dogs and cats. There was a picture of a bride embracing her maid of honor on the cover of the lifestyle section. The woman was dressed in an ivory gown with lace and beading while her German Shepherd sidekick wore a similar style in a contrasting shade of blue. While it didn't do much for her rugged complexion (the dog's not the bride's) she appeared to enjoy the attention.

All I could think was: I hope the groom knows what he is getting into. The bride and her four legged friend seemed to be enjoying an exclusive relationship. I couldn't help but wonder how the new husband would fit in or even *if* he would.

When our son tied the knot a few years ago, I wondered the same thing. His fiancé's 5 year old terrier had already experienced 5 years of "thick and thin" before Daniel ever entered the picture. I knew he was in trouble (our son, not the dog) when I learned that Caiden's food was made from scratch with organic ingredients. After 35 years of marriage, my husband wishes he had it so good.

According to the article, a significant portion of the "thirty-something" population is choosing to nurture canines instead of children. Hey, I get it. Dogs are cheaper, loyal to the core, and they don't talk back. Compare that to life with a surly teenager. No contest.

A couple of years after they married, our son and his wife adopted a second dog. Caiden, who has always acted more like a feline than a canine, now has a brother named Woody. The new guy is a 2 year old cocker spaniel they rescued from homelessness. Woody is adorable. He has eyelashes like a giraffe and velvety, oversized ears. There is not a discriminating bone in his body. He loves anyone with a pulse. Animal dander makes me itch and sneeze so I try to keep my distance. He won't have any of that. He trots over and sits at my feet. Then he rests his chin on my knee as if to say "I know you love me." When he looks at me with those big brown eyes, I do.

If only I believed in reincarnation, I would definitely come back as a dog. Perhaps I would enjoy life as a standard poodle. A weekly appointment at the groomers with the occasional visit to doggy yoga sounds like a life of luxury, don't you think? Did you know there is a hotel in Paris that offers VIP services for $400 a night? The *Very Important Pet* service includes a gourmet meal delivered by room service, unlimited games, a personal trainer, massage therapy and, of course, a designer doggy bed. If you want to indulge your pooch beyond that, diamond tiaras and jeweled necklaces are available for an additional fee. Nothing's too good for man's best friend.

When I think back on the life our dogs led, it makes me laugh. The way we treated them would probably get us in trouble with animal advocacy groups, these days. Our Golden Retrievers lived outside. When the weather was cold or rainy, we opened the door to the garage where two folded blankets waited for them on the concrete floor. On the rare days when they were invited inside, they knew their place. Climbing or sitting on furniture was strictly verboten. Jimmy and I discussed getting a puppy, but treating dogs like dogs is so "*nineties*". I think we'll just wait for the grandkids.

# GOLDEN GIRLS ENJOY
# GOLDEN TRIANGLE

I had been trying to get my mom and mother-in law-together for years. I knew they'd have a good time. Now in her early nineties, Reba prefers to stay home. Since Momma still travels, (she's only 89) we invited ourselves to the Crouch house. Last Friday, we zipped our toothbrushes into suitcases and pointed my Honda east.

I have spent hundreds of nights in the house where my husband grew up, but it was Momma's first overnight stay. Walking from one room to another, she couldn't stop talking about how cozy it felt. Seeing my mother-in-law's house through Momma's eyes put me in mind of my first visit there. As soon as I walked in, I knew I belonged there. It wasn't just the warmth of a well-loved home that felt right to me. It was Reba herself. When Jimmy popped the question, his mother closed the deal.

She is so much like my own mother, it amazes me. Both ladies grew up in the Golden Triangle-an area in southeast Texas. Both married WWII veterans who were older, taller and remarkably handsome. They each made it to their 40th wedding anniversaries and still live in the house where they raised their kids. Both chose full time motherhood and later, when their kids were older, worked to help build the family business. They have each buried a child. Through more adversity than either one cares to remember, they have each mastered the art of acceptance.

Last Saturday, while sitting with them at the kitchen table, I just watched. They sure didn't need me to keep the conversation going. Laughing about everything that came up, they were like college coeds catching up after summer break. With their freshly coifed silver curls, (they both enjoy standing salon appointments) they were the epitome of cute. I admit to being biased, so please don't take my word for it. Ask anyone in Applebee's where we ate dinner. That's where Reba takes all her house guests. She has her own booth by the window. From there, she can see the building where the family insurance agency used to be.

Our waitress was so enamored by my dinner companions that she almost forgot to take our order. Standing there with her pad and pen, she launched into a monologue about her Papaw and his penchant for Cajun cooking. "I'm still full from last night's fish fry", she boasted, patting her tummy. Honestly, I thought we'd never eat. I tapped my foot impatiently under the table. Reba just smiled and listened. That's her response whenever strangers engage her. With Momma, it's a different story.

My mother reaches out and touches people. Literally. Whenever she passes a baby on the street, she traces the sign of the cross on his forehead. During our dinner at Applebee's, she blessed more than one. Our evening out was quite entertaining. My two moms attracted people like bees to honey. On our way to the car, a grey haired man challenged Reba to a competition. "Wanna have a race?" he flirted as he rolled his walker past.

After dinner, we took a drive that triggered more stories. "Remember Pleasure Island?" Momma reminisced. She loves to talk about the early 1930s when she and her friends drove from one side of the golden triangle to the other for dances. There was something about the boys from Reba's town.

Next month, Reba will celebrate her 92nd birthday. A few days later Momma will turn 89. Yes, they share a zodiac sign, too. Maybe we'll throw them a joint birthday celebration. Their blue eyes lit up when I suggested it. These ladies love to party.

As the weekend drew to a close, they kept asking me, "Is today our last day?" It made me wonder why in the world I hadn't made this happen before. Was I concerned they would tire of each other? Or did I worry they would simply get tired? I should have known better. Like twins separated at birth, they brought out the best in each other. For the Golden Girls, the Golden Triangle was a good place to be.

# GRENADE IN THE GARDEN

I just returned from a weekend with Jimmy's family. His brother is happily married to a woman named Pam. Besides being my sister-in-law, she is also my friend. When she mentioned her plan to install plants in their backyard on Saturday, I offered to help. I don't happen to have a green thumb, but I am the proud owner of a very strong back. For some unknown reason, I find digging in the dirt therapeutic. Or maybe I'm hoping that if I hang out long enough with Pam, some of her horticultural skills will rub off on me.

We waited until the temperature dropped below 90 and then hauled our wheelbarrow of tools to the garden. We chatted as we worked side by side attacking the caliche with our sharpened hoes. We had high hopes of transforming that "hard as a rock" flower bed into a place where bushes and flowers might flourish. Crunch, crunch, crunch... and then clank! Out popped something that was not indigenous to the Texas landscape.

"Is that a grenade?" asked Pam.

"It sure looks like it," I said. Then I wracked my brain to figure out what battle had been fought in the Golden Triangle in the last century. Impulsively, I reached for the thing. Looking back, it seems foolish. What was I planning to do with it?

"Don't touch it, she yelled."Gunpowder never dies!" I have no idea how she knows such things, or if it's even true. Since she said it with such conviction, I didn't doubt it for one second. The next morning's headline flashed in my imagination: *Texan Woman maimed by a 75 year old hand grenade.* I jerked my hand back as fast as I could.

"What should we do?" I asked.

"We're calling 911," she said as she ran past me for her cell phone. In 10 minutes, three of the city's finest were on the scene. By now, the man of the house, Bryan, had joined our motley crew. "Do any of you have military experience?" he asked the guys in uniform. What a time to check credentials.

One of them answered, "He just got back from Iraq." He was pointing to the officer who was digging dirt from under the grenade with his ball point pen. I noticed it was a Bic. Not exactly the tool I would have expected. I began to eavesdrop on the officers' conversation. In less than 5 minutes the consensus had gone from "it's probably a toy" to "let's call Fort Polk." I dated a guy who was stationed there when I was in college. It's in Louisiana. According to the police chief, that base offered the most geographically desirable bomb experts.

As they were kicking around the idea of calling the bomb squad, 6 firemen pulled up in their truck. That brought our number of uniformed personel to 9. The curb in front of the house was filled with 2 police cars, a fire truck and an impressive looking Haz Mat unit. Neighbors were gathering, too.

Finally, without any fanfare, one of the men picked up the grenade with his bare hand. He turned it over. No pin. Or as the guy just back from Iraq put it, no "*spoon*." Just like the ones at Army Surplus, this grenade had been drilled out. The object of so much attention and concern was as hollow as the rotted out tree trunk next to it. Our excitement was over.

As we walked our community helpers back to their modes of transportation, the firemen started a new conversation. They figured out how much it had cost for 9 guys and 4 vehicles to "disarm" an empty grenade. I was shocked at the monumental waste of taxpayer's money. Pam was undaunted.

"I'd rather be safe than sorry," she muttered. With that, she walked back to the garden. An hour later, covered in sweat and grime, we were finished with our project. It was almost ten p.m. but the azalea bushes were in the ground. On the way back into the house, I stopped for a moment to gaze upon the gorgeous night sky. Given the events of the evening, I should have expected what I saw there, but it took me by surprise. The moon was completely full.

# HELPING MOMMA STAY PUT

Old age is not for the faint of heart. Just ask my 89-year-old mother. With every year that passes, she loses more of her freedom and independence. These are, not counting her children, the things she loves the most. She also loves her home. Staying there is her heart's desire. It's her children's hope for her to stay there, as well. It's like walking a tightrope to maintain the balance between keeping her safe and keeping her happy. When forced to pick one over the other, we choose to keep her safe.

Momma still lives in the house we grew up in. It's a two story traditional with all bedrooms upstairs. Over the past 6 decades, she has carved memories into every nook and cranny. So have her fourteen children, 39 grandchildren and 22 great grandchildren. To say we're attached to the century old homestead-our family headquarters- is an understatement of epic proportion. We love that place, cracks and all.

When Daddy died, more than twenty years ago, our oldest brother moved into the garage apartment behind the house. He promised our father on his death bed that he would look after Momma. That was long before she needed looking after. Now his presence on her property is making all the difference in her quality of life. He has become her cook, driver and most importantly, the administrator of her medicines.

After her last appointment, the doctor demanded that changes be made. He said that navigating stairs during the day and sleeping alone at night are no longer acceptable for someone in her age group. But she loves her house! What to do? A family meeting was called. "Operation Keep Momma Safe" was launched.

Here's what I can say about Momma. She does not give up without a fight. What did I think? That the woman who met the challenge of mothering so many would let anyone else tell her what to do? "If I fall down the stairs and die, so be it!" she said when I reminded her to hold the handrail. Unlike her doctor, she loves her stairs. She's convinced that going up and down steps all day is the reason her legs have stayed strong.

Until recently, she's been open to the prospect of moving to an assisted living facility. In fact, she's been enthusiastic about one place in particular. "When the time comes," she told us, "that's where I want to go." At the urging of her doctor, four of her daughters went to check it out. The grounds were covered with colorful flowers and lush foliage. Living there, she would eat three meals a day in a cheery dining room lined with big windows.

Enhanced by centerpieces and tablecloths, the cafeteria looked warm and inviting. However, in the event that Momma might not feel like being social, the kitchen could send dinner to her room. They have a computer room staffed with a technology teacher, a ballroom for holiday parties, and a chapel for daily Mass. How much would she love that?

Our final stop on the tour was the sunroom. That's the area where residents are encouraged to hang out with their friends. Stepping off the elevator, we walked by an elderly man napping on the couch. Upright but severely curved, his head was resting in his own lap. A few feet away, a white haired woman clutched a plastic doll. She rocked back and forth with a vacant gaze. Two ladies sat in overstuffed chairs looking out the window. Close enough to touch each other, they kept to their own separate worlds. Two women sitting side by side in complete silence? These people were not like Momma. I've often heard that elderly folks who are moved from their homes into facilities often go downhill soon after. Now I see why.

After our tour, *Operation: Keeping Momma Safe* became *Helping Momma Stay Put*. At the family meeting that same day, everybody offered to help. We checked off her doctor's orders like items on a grocery list. One brother will check in on her daily after dropping his wife at work. Two sisters committed to take early retirement so they can visit every few days. Brother who lives in her garage apartment will sleep in the house at night. There is a way for everyone to contribute. Momma hates the fact that we're in her business, but she loves that we're in her house. She also loves that we're helping her stay there.

# JUST SPEAK UP

"*Shoulda*", *woulda, coulda. My* ex-husband is in the trunk". I learned that expression from my friend, Virginia. An older and wiser next-door neighbor, she was my sounding board throughout early marriage struggles. The two of us laughed every time she uttered that phrase even though neither one knew what it meant. As is often the case with old adages, there was truth buried in it. The part that resonated loudest was "shoulda". As in, "I shoulda spoken up."

Last night, my six girlfriends and I went to see "Hope Springs". It was a movie about an older married couple, who had fallen, over the course of their long-term marriage into a deep rut. Both husband and wife knew they had settled for mediocrity. He was content to accept status quo whereas she longed for a "real marriage". The conflict began when she signed them up for a weeklong marital workshop. Almost trite, it's a common scenario that veteran couples can relate to. It sure struck a chord with me.

The kitchen scene that was played over and over for emphasis was my favorite of the entire movie. He walked in dressed for his day at the office, draped his jacket over the chair, placed his briefcase on the table and plopped down for breakfast. His dutiful wife put the same plate of fried cholesterol in front of him within moments of his arrival every morning. The film maker's message was clear. Their marriage was monotonous. That was obvious, but it triggered a question. Did that scene reflect a rut or a ritual?

Watching the characters plod through their uninspired life together, I realized something. It's not the sameness that takes us down. Routine can serve married life like backbone serves the body. It holds the thing together. Doing the same rituals can actually provide warmth and comfort. Like a wool coat on a wintry day. No, it's not routine that sours relationships. It's the expectations that are left unspoken.

When my sister, Candy, was in high school, she had a serious boyfriend. Like most serious boyfriends, he hung around our house a lot. In his frequent visits, he observed that Candy had to wait for her turn under the family hairdryer. Five sisters wearing giant brush rollers were in line for that plastic bonnet and hose contraption every Friday night. So many heads of hair sharing one appliance made getting to the football game before kickoff almost impossible.

What did he do? He marched right over to Sears and bought her a hair dryer of her very own. I watched him give it to her, a big smile on his face. She ripped off the wrapping paper and burst into tears. It turns out she had her heart set on a charm bracelet. He didn't know. Four years younger and still in the throes of adolescence, I didn't understand her reaction any more than he did. If she wanted something so much, why hadn't she spoken up about it?

After getting married, I asked myself the same question. It's like we expect our loved ones to read our minds. When we live under the same roof, sleep in the same bed and breathe the same air, it's tempting to expect a spouse to know our wants and needs. That's what I called romance. I thought it would grace my marriage like April showers on spring flowers.

But men are from Mars and women are from Venus, remember? So what have I learned in 35 years? If I want to have something or go somewhere especially if he doesn't share my enthusiasm for that something, I have learned to use specific language. "I really want to go. Will you go with me?" It sounds ridiculously simple, but the words are like magic. He rarely says no to requests like that because I don't make them very often. In fact, I use this "code" very sparingly. An interesting thing happened when I started speaking up for what I really wanted. I started getting a lot more of it.

I don't want a mind reader for a husband. I want a husband who listens and cares. Isn't that what everybody in relationship wants from each other? But more than that, I want to be a better listener. I'm betting that if couples learn to speak up and tune in, romance will follow quite naturally. At least, it's worth talking about.

# KIDS SAY THE DARNEDEST THINGS

Kids say the darnedest things. There used to be a television show by that name. Baby boomers remember it was hosted by a personality named Art Linkletter. Art was an expert in tickling kids' funny bones. Between his talent for discovering extraverted children and their innate disregard for etiquette, the live interviews were good for a giggle. Last week at work, I felt like a host on that show.

My friend, who owns a child development center found herself short-staffed. I told her I had been thinking of getting back into the classroom. She asked me if I'd like to do some substitute teaching. "It will be a good way to test the waters," she suggested. So I donned a T-shirt, jeans and tennis shoes (I learned the hard way to wear nothing but washable cotton around four year olds and finger paint) and struck out for school.

Like any job, my new position came with a learning curve. Remembering schedules, getting to know fellow workers, and learning all the children's names were the hard parts. It took awhile to embrace my new culture and I came home every day totally spent. I told myself that working 9-6 with 3-5 year olds would sap anyone's strength. The truth is, after sitting out for a year, I was "off my game".

Recess meant an hour on the playground with 2 other teachers and thirty little ones. There were no benches in sight, so I found a railroad tie, sat down and began to supervise play time. Four-year-old Gwyneth was the first to approach me. She stood so close I could feel her breath. As she stared at me with her big brown eyes, I felt like an animal on exhibit. I guess I was to her.

At four years of age, kids rarely understand the concept of personal space. I smiled, put my hands around each of her little arms and gently moved her back six inches. It's flu season, after all. But it was no use. She couldn't keep her pudgy fingers off my turquoise necklace. Note to self: leave the necklaces at home.

Wearing jewelry to teach pre-k and expecting little girls to keep their hands off is like leaving them in a candy shop unattended and expecting them not to snitch the gumdrops. "Where do you live?" she asked. "Where's your daddy?" She fired the questions at me quickly. Her interrogation skills were like a police investigator. I tried to answer her queries and protect my string of stones. It wasn't easy.

Unlike adults, little ones are not one bit concerned with social etiquette. They want what they want. This one's mission was to "vet" me and she was entirely focused on her work. Thank God, the director hadn't been as scrutinizing during my job interview. I probably wouldn't have made the cut. The curly haired brunette stared at me without expression. I couldn't tell if I was passing her test or not. Finally, she abandoned me for her friends who called her from the play house.

Suddenly, Max and Mary Claire were standing in her place. I shook my head. Where did they come from? "He took my shovel," said Mary Claire, real tears pooling in her eyes. "She hit me with it," he said, holding up the red spade. Ah, an arbitration opportunity! Finally, something I can sink my "teacher teeth" into. I gathered my most basic conflict resolution skills and attempted to help them find agreement. It went pretty well if I do say so myself. They raced back to the sand box after promising to take turns with the shovel.

All in all, it was a busy week. Low man on the totem pole, I had been responsible for sponging down tables after snack, sweeping up cracker crumbs and setting out and picking up the cots for nap time. Convincing the "older fours" most of whom have outgrown the need for a daily nap to stay on their pillows for two hours took some creativity. However, the rest of my job description didn't offer any mental challenge at all. In fact, part of the day had been downright boring. I was trying to figure out where the teaching part of this position was hiding when a more puzzling question popped into my head.

Why did I like it?

Then Kaitlin came running over, her blonde braids hanging lopsided behind her ears. "You're the best new teacher ever!" she announced. "Will you read us another story when we go back inside?" Kids say the darnedest things. I'll be back on Monday.

# TEXAS LANDSCAPE
# MIRRORS MARRIAGE

What better excuse for a road trip than a family wedding? As soon as the embossed invitation hit our respective mailboxes, my sister and I started discussing the possibility. One might think that saving a thousand dollars in airfare would be reason enough for our spouses to agree. But seventeen hours in a vehicle over the course of one weekend is not an easy sell. Getting the guys to jump on the bandwagon, or in this case the SUV, would surely take some doing.

So we reminded them of the advantage of having our own car once we got there and followed that up with the falling gas prices. In the end, the ability to keep our shoes on is what convinced our hubbies to drive instead of fly. We packed the car and headed west for a city that lies on the edge of Texas: El Paso.

It was so early when we struck out on our adventure, the hill country sky was still pink. On country roads that wound through small towns, we marveled at hundred year old town halls and quaint store fronts. Oohing and aahing like tourists in Europe, my sister and I were having a ball. Our husbands sat in front programming the GPS while we settled ourselves in the back with an Atlas spread across our laps.

Before we knew it, we were halfway there. An 80 mile an hour speed limit helped and so did the scenery. We were lifted up by rolling hills and limestone cliffs. But Texas is big and the outdoor scene changed as we rolled along. Glistening lakes under a pastel sky gave way to scrub brush, parched land and craggy rocks. It made me think of marriage. One day can be thrilling, euphoric even. Like the feeling one has after climbing to the top of a mountain. The next day can be just the opposite, leaving one as parched as a wanderer in a sun drenched desert.

My sister and her husband were high school sweethearts. Together since the 60s, they can't imagine life without each other. She also can't resist backseat driving. "Better stop for gas," she said. "It might be our last chance for awhile". He shook his head. "I have it under control," he answered. You worry too much." These awkward exchanges are no big deal. Jimmy and I have our differences, too. He likes to get "in the zone" when he drives. I like to talk while we roll along. Cindy and I chatted most of the way. Let's just say that everyone was more than ready for a bit of space and freedom by the time we pulled up to the hotel.

We dressed up for the wedding, but no one held a candle to the bride and groom's glamour. Tall, dark and elegant, she floated down the aisle like an angel dressed in lace. He looked heavenly, too. His big white smile lit up the church. When they met up on the altar, we could feel their excitement. And then the minister's words brought everyone back to earth. "There will be a day," he said, "when storms will come. The storms of life hit everybody".

I squeezed Jimmy's hand. We have weathered a few. What exactly was it that kept us together? I'm not sure, but staying has been its own reward. Will the kids who are in tonight's spotlight make it last? They both grew up in long term marriages- thirty years for each of their parents. Hopefully, they learned a thing or two from their role models.

At the end of the weekend, we packed once again and steeled ourselves for the long trip ahead. There were 8 ½ hours between us and home sweet home. I dug for the car keys, but they were not where I put them. "How could you lose the car keys?" asked Jimmy. I finally found them but not before we squabbled a bit. It was a little embarrassing but better than the old days. Back then, it would have gotten really ugly. Tolerance has been the key to our marriage turnaround. I am learning to accept and tolerate what happens, since I can't control the storms of life.

On the way home, we passed the Sierra Blanca mountain one more time. The wind turbines waved us back through Fort Stockton like old friends. If we keep our eyes open, the drive through the heart of Texas offers plenty of beauty. It's the same for relationships, if we only keep looking. Like Lone Star landscape, an enduring marriage has more peaks than valleys.

# LAUGHING LIKE LIFE
# DEPENDS ON IT

Humor is huge on my mother's side of the family. If they can't solve a problem, they laugh it to death. Momma and her sisters have a genetic predisposition to the giggles. Aunt Polly, who lives in Utah, came to see us recently. With 7 kids who live all over the country, she spends most of her frequent flyer miles traveling to see offspring. On the rare occasion when she touches down in Texas, her sister's family comes running. Momma, especially, drops everything.

At 85, Polly no longer drives. She relies on her State of Utah identification card to get her on airplanes. While filling out her renewal form at the DPS the other day, she hit a snag. How to describe her current hair color? "It's not really blond", she admitted. "But it's definitely not grey." Her son, who had driven her on the errand leaned in for a closer look at her coiffure. "Cream?" he offered.

That's what she wrote down only to be corrected by the women behind the counter. "Cream is not a color." She had to step out of line and start over with a new form. It was a hassle that would have brought out the worst in most people. This blue eyed octogenarian just laughed when she told her story. "I guess people with cream hair pose a threat to national security."

Apparently, their father (known as Papaw to the grandkids) loved a good joke, too. He used to read articles aloud from the morning newspaper as the family sat around the breakfast table. He plugged his daughters' names into the articles and read them aloud. "Singer-songwriter Polly Phelan is the biggest success story of this year's Grammy Awards". "Congratulations to Officer Donia Phelan of the Beaumont Police Department who singlehandedly captured the Montclair cat burglar." The more ridiculous he sounded, the more they giggled.

I can relate to that sort of nonsense. Three of my nine sisters spent the night at our house last Saturday night. They were in town for a friend's art exhibition. We treated ourselves to an old fashioned slumber party. It had been a while since we'd been altogether, so we changed into our jammies and stayed up till 1 a.m. Our kids range in age from 24 to 38. We spent much of the night discussing the blessings and curses of motherhood. It seems the heavier the topic, the darker our humor and the louder our laughter. We tried to keep our voices down out of respect for my sleeping husband. That reminded me of our growing up years with Daddy. On school nights, we closed the bedroom door and buried our faces in our pillows, so he couldn't hear us. He did not appreciate our late night shenanigans. Daddy's sense of humor ran out at ten o'clock on weeknights and midnight on weekends.

Jimmy enjoys it when my sisters come to visit because he loves them. He also sees how much fun we have together. But he doesn't begin to understand our brand of humor. At the above mentioned slumber party, Cindy and I stood in the kitchen with the pantry door open for a good 15 minutes. We were trying to decide whether to bake the German Chocolate or Double Dutch Fudge cake mix. After serious deliberation, we opened both boxes and dumped them into the same bowl. For some reason we found that hilarious. We collapsed on the floor with tears running down our faces." Jimmy just stared. Then he walked into the bedroom and closed the door behind. We found that funny, too.

I guess you had to be there. A shared childhood has bound us together, but it's the laughter that keeps us coming back for more. We can't seem to get enough "doubled over, shoulder-shaking belly laughs". Momma and her sisters have taught us well. Their legacy of laughter will live on. "She Never Took Herself Seriously" would make a fitting epitaph for the Phelan girls.

It's been said a million times. Laughter is the best medicine. Perhaps that's why Momma and her eighty something sister don't take handfuls of pills every day like some of their peers. So far, their golden years are full of monkey business and packed with fun. May they laugh for the rest of their days and when those days run out, may they die laughing.

# LEARNING A NEW LANGUAGE
# AFTER SAYING I DO

My husband and I don't speak the same language. At least we didn't when we got married. We communicated perfectly throughout our courtship and honeymoon stages, but that was when our words floated out to each other on clouds of euphoria. In the beginning, expressing ourselves was effortless. It was about the time our first child was born that messages started getting lost in translation.

Jimmy speaks a language of facts and worst case scenarios. He is a problem solver. The challenge of finding a solution for every possibility is what gets him out of bed in the morning. I am an optimist. A cheerful person by nature, I can't stand negativity. In my husband's eyes, I am a Pollyanna who avoids reality whenever I can.

My job is to lift him up. His job is to keep me grounded. You can see that we are well suited for each other. Theoretically, I am the yin to his yang. However, in reality, we don't understand each other a lot of the time. In other words, we don't speak the same language.

In this we are not unique. Opposites often attract. There are probably more couples that match our profile than otherwise. So what do we do when communication is difficult? We learn a new language. If we pay close attention, we can learn the vocabulary of our spouses. Case in point: every Saturday morning, Jimmy gets up and washes clothes, cuts the grass and vacuums the cars. Then he collapses on the couch in front of whatever sporting event is on. At that point, it's about noon so I call to him from the kitchen, "Would you like a sandwich?"

I know what he likes for lunch. It's a ham and cheese on wheat, slathered with mustard and mayonnaise, pepper sprinkled generously on the mayo. But instead of asking for that, he says, "I'll get something in a minute." For years, I took him at his word. He would saunter into the kitchen ten minutes later as I put the finishing touches on my grilled chicken salad. As soon as I left the kitchen counter, he began to assemble the above mentioned sandwich.

One day I realized what was going on. He wanted the sandwich but he didn't want to ask me to make the sandwich. For whatever reason, it was okay for me to cook dinner every night, but he didn't feel right about lunch on the weekends. Maybe his mom didn't make sandwiches for his dad. Who knows?

Once I broke the code, the rest was easy. I asked him if he wanted a sandwich, he said he'd get it. I made it, anyway. He ate it. Easy, breezy. We bring a lot of strange behavior to our relationships. Our "family of origin" baggage is packed to overflowing when we get married. Finding our way to a happy marriage involves learning what to respond to and what to ignore. In fact, learning how to keep our mouths shut is key. My sister actually puts her hand over her mouth when she feels a tacky comment coming.

I've come a long way in breaking down the "Jimmy Code". I have learned that he likes to unload the dishwasher but he prefers a little help with the process. If I happen to be in the kitchen when the dishes are clean and cooled, I stand in front of one cabinet and let him hand those dishes to me. A small thing, sure, but it makes him feel supported.

He has learned that I would rather watch a chick flick at home with him than spend the evening in a fancy restaurant. He also knows by now that holding my hand while we're out in public makes me feel loved. For a man who doesn't care much for public displays of affection, it's not important. To me, it's huge.

It boils down to paying attention. To stay in touch with one's partner we must learn as much about each other as we can. It's hard enough to get along when people speak the same language. Stumbling along in a relationship without fluency is like getting by on crackers when you could feast on filet mignon. Be willing to learn a new vocabulary. It will speak volumes about your love.

# LIFE IS PRECIOUS,
# HANDLE WITH LAUGHTER

Sometimes I wake up inspired.

Every once in a while I am blessed with an idea that I have to write down before I even get out of bed. That is what happened this morning. It wasn't a dream either. It was simply a persistent notion that came to me as soon as I opened my eyes. Glimpsing out the window at a still dark sky, I reached for my notebook before the train of thought left the station. Ready? Here it is.

*Life is precious.*

I know. It's not exactly a profound thought, but it resonated loudly with me this morning. Perhaps that's because of the devastating losses our family has suffered over the past few months. As the year comes to a close, I can't wait to toss the 2011 kitchen calendar into the trash can. Two family members died this year. Neither one of them was even old yet.

Shelly, my best friend since high school, died on the slopes during a skiing vacation. One minute she was fit as a fiddle and chatting with her friends at the top of the run. In the next, she was face down in the snow. It was a massive aneurysm. According to her traveling buddies, she hadn't complained of a headache or pain of any sort. In fact, she had just expressed a desire for mussels and chardonnay, her favorite lunch. By the time the ski patrol arrived, she wasn't breathing.

When I say that Shelly left a hole in my life the size of Texas, I am not exaggerating. Besides being my best friend, she was the most entertaining person I've ever met. She brought out the funniest part of me, too. Besides my husband, she knew me better than anyone. Here's how long we have been best friends. We met before the Beatles got famous.

Whenever we were together, belly laughs were a given. It didn't matter where we were, we had a wonderful time. Once, when I came to stay with her, she talked me into going to a friend's funeral. I didn't even know the man, so it seemed highly inappropriate. Pulling a black dress out of her closet, she convinced me that it was the right thing to do. It's embarrassing to admit, but we actually had a fun time there, too.

Shelly taught me quite a bit. The most important thing of all was not to take myself so seriously. It was something I needed to learn. Being raised by an angry dad left me thinking I had to be perfect. Especially as a young mother, I was intense. "Lighten up, Doni," she said many times. And then she'd flash her million dollar smile and I knew she was right.

The other person in our family circle who died last year was Bryan. Like Shelly, he had a great sense of humor and he died well before his time. Unlike Shelly, his death was neither sudden nor surprising. The cancer took a year to claim him. He passed away in early June, just before the Texas heat drove us inside for the summer.

The last good time we had together was in his backyard. From his hammock in the shade, he teased me about my questionable gardening skills. I didn't even know there was a right way to hold a spade. Bryan died ten days after his wife and I installed those daisies along the fence line. He was funny until the end.

I have been told that it's the difficult family members who make the best teachers. Perhaps it's because they force us to learn tolerance. That could be so, but I think the best instructors are the ones who show us how to laugh at ourselves, no matter what the circumstances. If that's true, Shelly and Bryan were masters in their crafts.

There is no doubt about it, the year 2011 was hell on earth. I cried my way through it but my heart tells me there is more where that came from. All the more reason to practice the lessons they taught me. Life is precious. Handle with laughter.

# LOADING UP ON LOVE

I love February. Who would guess a month so short could be so action packed? The month has something for everyone. The Super Bowl offers football junkies the ultimate fix. Confetti from that event is still in the grass when the Mardi Gras floats start rolling in: "Throw me something, Mister!" can be heard all up and down the Gulf coast. And then, finally, drum roll please, Valentine's Day! Did you know it's the number two holiday in the world? This sweetheart of a celebration plays second fiddle only to New Year's.

Retailers are masters at capitalizing on Valentine's global popularity. They hang shiny, red hearts all over the stores even before January's white sales are over. The first month of the year gets very little respect. The opening scene is lit with fireworks, but by the end of her days, she has nothing to show for her efforts but recycled resolutions soon to be forgotten.

But that's a subject for another column. Today's message is reserved for the greatest emotion of them all and the month that serves it up. How do I love thee, February? Let me count the ways. I love the plethora of greeting cards that seem written just for me. I love the fancy flowers that wither and die within days of delivery and the creamy chocolates that guarantee I will gain those same 3 pounds it took a month to lose. Valentine's Day has kept Cupid busy since time began.

She is the quintessential ruler of romance. I am among her most loyal subjects.

As much as I love candle lit dinners for two, it seems unfair that couples have all the fun. Isn't it politically incorrect, in this era of inclusivity, to stamp Valentine's Day with nothing but romance when there are so many other kinds of love to be enjoyed? What about agape, better known as selfless love. And then there is fraternal, platonic and let's not forget the mother of them all: Unconditional love. Shouldn't Valentine's Day make room in its program for every kind of love?

I'm still riding an emotional high from the family meeting we had last week. As we planned the gathering to discuss our aging mother, sibling emails flew back and forth like arrows aimed at a moving target. With so many siblings, (13 of us looking for consensus on Momma's care and safety) and different opinions in the mix, I worried that our get-together would be argumentative and disagreeable.

I was wrong. Instead of discord, harmony filled the air. We started with a prayer and ended with champagne. Somehow in the midst of all the strong willed people, love conquered all. I'm still not sure how, but during those two hours in my little sister's living room, we found our way to common ground.

Now, infused with fraternal love, I'm giving advice where none has been solicited. If you have a beef with a sibling, get over it. You might say it's none of my business, but if our supersized, opinionated set of siblings can put aside differences, so can yours.

Let's dedicate this Valentine's Day to the kind of love that keeps families talking. There is no room in this short and sweet month for holding grudges against anyone, especially kinfolk. If you are "out of relationship" with a brother, sister, mother, father, cousin, or nephew, fix it. Stores are stocked floor to ceiling during the month of February with heart shaped gifts that would make perfect peace offerings. Send wine, flowers, chocolates or maybe just a heart-felt note. If you can't figure out what to say, let Hallmark do it for you. All You Need Is Love.

The Beatles didn't coin that phrase. They just put the words to a catchy tune and made a hit song out of it. All You Need Is Love? I used to think that sentence was an overgeneralization. Now I think it's the most profound truth of all. *All You Need Is Love!* And there are so many ways to get it. Thanks, February for serving up a holiday that works for absolutely everyone. Happy Valentine's Day!

# LOVE COVERS EVERYTHING

I can see the past from here.

If I stand in a certain place on our back deck and look into our neighbor's yard, it's like watching a movie of our children growing up. A family of five lives next door. Dad is the economic anchor, Mom is the primary caregiver, and there are three kids: two boys and a girl. Aside from being twenty years younger, they are our family's mirror image. It's the same dynamic, the same family culture, the same religion. Even our personalities are similar. Sometimes, when they are out in the backyard together, the words that float across the fence are downright nostalgic.

"Mom, they won't let me play!" That's the plaintive cry of the 5-year-old daughter. She is the only girl and the baby of the family. Just like our daughter, she is a few years younger than her two brothers. Big surprise: her male siblings don't always include her in their fun. How well I remember that. "Let her play," I insisted when our daughter whined of being left out. In retrospect, I realize I may have stuck my nose in where it didn't belong once or twice. Ya think?

All these years later, a thought occurs. If offered a do over, would I take it? Would I go back to those days, if I thought I could do better the second time around? My sister Judi and I often discuss our misguided parenting styles, since we raised our children in similar fashion.

Were the challenges that our children encountered upon reaching adulthood the result of things we did or things we didn't do? Did we make life too easy? Did we rescue them too often?

One thing is for sure. These questions never crossed our parents' minds. Their parenting was sure-footed and disciplined. They told us kids no on a regular basis and we never argued. Daddy had his faults. Being overly soft was certainly not one of them. "Because I said so" was a good enough reason for anything. It never occurred to most of us (there were a few rebels in our bunch who had more guts than Judi and I) to test his authority. Sometimes, when I hear little kids talking back to their fathers in public, I gasp. Then I try to imagine saying that to Daddy. The idea is so preposterous, it makes me laugh.

Another parenting difference between us and our folks was the way we involved ourselves in our kids' school projects. Momma didn't even think about helping us. With fourteen kids, she probably realized it was a practice that would never end, once begun. "Hands off" would have been our mother's philosophy no matter how many children she was rearing. They were *our* assignments, therefore *our* responsibilities.

For whatever reason, I helped my children a whole lot more than our mother helped me. I'm thinking back on all the midnight oil I burnt in front of that clunky desktop computer editing essays that were due the next morning. Even at the time, I suspected I was overparenting, but I couldn't bring myself to say no. If I hadn't figured it out on my own, our firstborn son clarified things after he went off to college. "I wish you hadn't bailed me out so much in high school," he said.

There it is. In retrospect, WWII parents might have operated at a distance, but there's no doubt about it, baby boomer parents hovered way too close. Last time I looked, the pendulum was still swinging, but the question persists. Would I want to go back and correct my mistakes? I don't think so. I did the best I could at the time. There is no such thing as perfect parenting. What matters is that our kids know we love them. My mother said it often while we were growing up. *Love covers over a multitude of sins.* It is all that matters.

# LOVING WITHOUT STRINGS

I'm lucky. I was born to a good mother. Then I married Jimmy and my lucky star of motherhood burned even more brightly. None of those tacky jokes apply to my mother-in-law. She is as easy to love as my own mom and with good reason. These two women are like sisters separated at birth. They never take themselves seriously. They both keep their noses out of other people's business. Giving advice only when asked for it, they never criticize. Neither one of them ever learned how to lay guilt on their kids. Best of all, they know how to love unconditionally.

Coming from a family of 14, I had plenty of practice changing diapers and rocking babies before I had my own. I was nine years old when my youngest sibling was born. As soon as she came home from the hospital, I dubbed myself her primary caregiver. Forget Chatty Cathy, I had a living doll. With fair skin, dark hair and blue eyes, she looked just like the beauty in my favorite story book, "Snow White".

Seeing to the care and feeding of my little sister offered me plenty of useful experience. However, it didn't teach me a thing about loving unconditionally. Perhaps parenthood is a pre-requisite for that. But even after becoming a parent, loving without strings doesn't always come naturally. It is a generosity of Spirit that some parents have to cultivate. Mr. Rogers had it right.

"I love you just the way you are" is what every child needs to hear. When the kids were little, our television was tuned to that cardigan-clad wise man every day. Somehow, I didn't get the message.

During our first born son's senior year of high school, he and I had a power struggle. I wanted him to wash his clothes when he got home from school or on the weekends like normal people. He preferred the procrastination method: throwing them into the washing machine on school mornings at the very last moment. The first time he did it, I shook my head. "Those will never be dry in time for class". I was right, but that didn't matter one bit to him. He pulled them from the Kenmore, shook out the excess water and shimmied right into those soaking wet pants. Here's the kicker. He managed to get himself to school before the late bell rang. When he came home that afternoon, I asked him, "How can you concentrate wearing a wet pair of blue jeans?" He just shrugged, "They were dry before the end of first period."

Instead of fighting over such a silly thing, I should have laughed. My mentors surely would have. When the kids were little and I needed a love lesson, I buckled them into the Suburban and zipped down I-10 for a few days of enlightenment. With one pit stop, we arrived at Gran's house or Mamaw's by mid-afternoon. The rules at their homes were simple. If it wasn't immoral, illegal or dangerous, it was okay. One of the children's favorite pastimes when visiting Mamaw Reba was wriggling up the living room door frame to sit in the transom, an opening at the top of the door. To put it simply, she let them climb the walls.

Loneliness often comes with growing older. The matriarchs in our family haven't learned the meaning of that word yet and I'm wondering if their unconditional loving may have something to do with that. At 89 and 92, they get plenty of company. While they have relinquished their car keys, the traffic through their front doors remains a steady flow. Apparently, kids who grow up feeling unconditional love keep coming back for more. That's a fact we can count on. If that isn't enough reason to practice the art of unconditional loving, I don't know what is.

Happy Mother's Day to every mother everywhere. May we learn to love abundantly without a single string attached.

# MAKING LIFE COUNT
# AFTER THE LIMELIGHT

I love the Olympics. Sitting in front of the television screen with friends and family for a night of athletic performances is hard to pass up. When those games come around every four years, they are our viewing priority. I've always been a sucker for the thrill of victory and the agony of defeat.

The gymnasts are especially captivating . When they aren't center stage, I tune in for the swimming, volleyball and synchronized diving competitions. I am fascinated by the strength of spirit that propels these kids beyond their bodies. And then there are the swimmers. In 2012, did you see the American teenagers who swam back to back races and still managed to secure the gold? They were like fish! Or maybe it's just their determination that seemed inhuman.

And speaking of determination. Were you watching when Jordyn Wieber, the reigning world champion gymnast realized she had not qualified for the Olympic all-around competition? Even with her face in her hands, she couldn't hide her devastation. A few nights later, her radiant countenance told a different story. She helped the Fab Five flip and fly past the competition to win gold for the American team.

Later, as I watched her pull for her teammates from the stands, I couldn't help but wonder. What will she do after leaving the limelight? For that matter, what does any Olympian do when his career is over? Will he become a spokesperson? A coach? Will she work for Nike?

Our son, Will, played for the University of Texas baseball team during the 2005 season. It was an exciting time. They won the College World Series that year. Hitting a single, a double and a home run in the final game, Will contributed significantly. American teams that win national championships usually get invited to the White House. Will and his fellow team members looked forward to flying to Washington to accept congratulations from the president of the United States. However, due to complications from Hurricane Katrina that year, President Bush was unable to make it happen.

Seven years later, the baseball team finally got its moment in the sun. No longer the sitting president, President George W. Bush graciously welcomed them to his Dallas office. After shaking hands and posing for photographs, he shared stories about his time in office. Will said it was fun to hear his colorful anecdotes, but it was this paraphrased advice that left the biggest impression on him.

*No matter how great our accomplishments, we don't get to rest on our laurels.*

*What are you guys going to do to keep being useful?*

Most of the young men on the 2005 Championship team grew up dreaming about playing major league ball. Some made it to "The Bigs". Some played in the minors. Will traveled with the Arizona Diamondback farm team for awhile. When his baseball dream came to an end, it wasn't easy to let go. He needed a new challenge. Now, focused on business, he has one.

I guess if anyone has earned the right to rest on his laurels, it might be an ex-president. But like he told the guys, President Bush has no desire to "fritter away" the rest of his life. Sixteen years as governor of Texas and President of the United States, and these days he is busier than ever. When he hosted the team, he had just returned from Zambia where he and Laura painted a health clinic for African women.

*What are you guys going to do to keep being useful?* It's a good question.

My brother-in-law asked himself the same thing. For almost 30 years, he investigated epidemics all over the world. Then he retired from the Center for Disease Control. One week he attended his retirement party. The next week he started over doing almost the same thing.

Whether we are athletes, world leaders, epidemiologists, teachers or writers, everybody finds himself at the end of a road. The question is what to do when we get there.

# MARKING MILESTONES WITH
# FRIENDS AND STRANGERS

It's 10 am and I'm high as a kite. I've had three cups of coffee, but it's not the caffeine that has me revved up. My husband and I just passed a major milestone. Who knew that being married for 35 years would warrant this kind of celebration? I feel like a rock star.

It all started last Monday. We woke up to a call of congratulations from our children. It was the anniversary of that day in 1977 when Jimmy and I said "I do". No big deal to us, right? We expect our marriage to last. In our kids' opinion, 35 years of togetherness is something to crow about. They surprised us with an overnight stay in a hotel just a few miles from our house.

We usually celebrate with a simple dinner at our favorite restaurant. We exchange romantic greeting cards and sometimes I get flowers but that is the extent of it. There was a time when my hubby showed his feelings for me with shiny things in velvet boxes. However, it's been awhile since he succumbed to such extravagance. We agreed, at some point during our second decade, to give each other presents of a more practical nature. This year he bought me a wheelbarrow. I gave him sheets; Egyptian cotton no less. We were tickled with our treasures.

Yes, we're practical to a fault. So when our daughter-in-law proposed that we spend the night in a fancy hotel, we hesitated. It seemed silly to spend their money that way, especially considering those new sheets on our bed. Thank God we decided not to rain on her parade. Instead, we said, "Thank You!"

Our anniversary fell on a Monday, so we booked our sleepover for the following Saturday. A week of anticipation had an unexpected effect. I found myself getting more excited by the day. In fact, I talked about it to everyone. Every store clerk, friend and stranger got to hear about our festive plans. "We just had our 35th wedding anniversary!" I exclaimed. "We're going to a hotel to celebrate!" Even to my own ears, I sounded like a 5-year-old anticipating my birthday party. Apparently, enthusiasm is contagious. Everyone seemed thrilled for our good fortune.

Upon arriving at the hotel, our aura of excitement continued. Perfect strangers fawned over us; They were delighted that we had stayed married and were still smiling. Counting the chef at the breakfast buffet who left his omelets to offer congratulations, ten staff members sang their praises. Jimmy isn't crazy about the idea of attention from perfect strangers. He quickly grew weary of it. I soaked it up like a sponge.

It was as if we had blinking buttons pinned to our lapels. Wherever we went: the pool, the workout room, the café; there was someone waiting to share our occasion. I started handing over my phone so they would take our photo. This experience was worth documenting. The bellboy and the hostess were happy to accommodate me.

Google says that only 20 percent of married couples make it to their 35th wedding anniversary. I guess that's why people seemed so excited. Except for determination, we had no more going for us than some who end up in divorce court. I'm wondering if our sustained relationship could have anything to do with the fact that we continued to celebrate along the way?

We've certainly had our share of struggles. As we headed toward our twentieth year, we didn't even like each other very much. In an effort to recommit to each other, we decided to renew our vows. What started out as a simple re-enactment with our pastor and immediate family, quickly morphed into a houseful of close friends and some really good gumbo. I wore my wedding dress, yellowed with age. Jimmy wore a tux jacket and Bermuda shorts. We may have looked better back in 1977, but whatever we lacked in appearance, we made up for in experience.

Sharing that evening with loved ones was the shot in the arm we needed. It was our way of saying, "Yes, we still want this!" in front of witnesses. Wedding anniversaries are not to be taken lightly. The kids were right. Whether it's with friends or strangers, a 35th anniversary is worth celebrating.

# MOMMA'S MEDITATION

Looking out the window onto our backyard this morning, all I could see was a big brown mess. Soggy leaves had taken over the backyard during the winter months. Like most folks, we don't spend much time in our backyard until the weather warms up. Keeping it raked is not a high priority.

But now that spring is upon us, I can't wait to clean the place up. I want to pull up the things that froze over the winter. I want to prune back the dead branches. But most of all, I want to sweep away the leaves and pollen.

In the spring, we like to drink coffee on the deck in the morning. My girlfriends and I enjoy tea parties with a backdrop of chirping birds and tinkling wind chimes. When friends come over for dinner, I like to serve al fresco under the bistro lights that hang from the oak trees. But right now I wouldn't serve a dog out there.

In my opinion, there is only one way to clean the place up. The old fashioned way- sweeping. My husband doesn't understand why I would choose an antiquated piece of equipment when I could do the job in half the time with his "Sear's Special" leaf blower. That high-pitched machine is his choice for clearing every surface from the roof to the driveway. He'd probably use it for the kitchen if I didn't protest.

The whining noise drives me mad, but there's a bigger reason I choose a broom over blowing. There is something attractive about that back and forth motion. It's like the difference between tapping out a note by email and penning a letter in long hand. So what if it requires more time and effort? The payoff is worth it.

When we were growing up, Momma carried her long handled broom to the front porch every evening after dinner. She took her time sweeping the sidewalk that wrapped around our house on the corner. She swept the front porch every evening, too. When I first noticed her nightly ritual, I thought it seemed a bit obsessive. It was not at all like our mother to be so invested in neatness and order. And then one day it occurred to me. A woman with so many children surely craves time and space to herself. It was rarely available to her during the day, so when Daddy came home, she knew exactly where to go for quiet. None of us would follow her out the front door after dinner. There was always the chance she might put us to work.

Now that I'm a mother, I can imagine what she pondered while she swept. She probably planned her next project. What chair to reupholster or what wall to paint next? I bet she prayed, too because she always seemed more peaceful when she came back in the house from her evening escapes. The simple rhythm of sweeping the sidewalk yielded a measure of tranquility.

I must be like my mother because sweeping does the same for me. Not the least bit interested in efficiency, I prefer tasks that take more time than skill. My mind gets cleared along with the surface I tend. Like Momma, I sometimes use my quiet time to talk to God. Sometimes I use it to discern my next writing assignment. When ideas flutter down during my Momma Meditation", I sweep them up just like the leaves from all those oak trees.

Motherhood is hectic for everyone. Whether a mom has fourteen kids or three, we best find our peace wherever we can. Stretching, doing yoga, reading scripture, or sitting still; all of these have been known to soothe one's spirit. I like sweeping. It doesn't require quiet or solitude. It's a meditation that can happen anywhere and it's the only one I learned from Momma.

# MOTHERS DO WHAT
# NEEDS DOING

The months leading up to our daughter's wedding generated many blessings and a couple of surprises. The biggest blessing and surprise was her decision to forego the purchase of a new wedding veil to wear the one my mother made for me. Somehow, the crown of tulle and lace that has been folded over a wire hanger for 34 years, still looked pretty good. In fact, when the bride-to-be wore it around the salon on the day we shopped for wedding gowns, a couple of fellow shoppers left their pedestals for a closer look.

"Where did you find that?" asked one girl. "Is there another one like it?"

I was delighted with her attraction to it and downright shocked at other brides' interest. However, upon closer inspection, I realized it would require a bit of fluffing. So I rinsed it in warm, sudsy water and hung it outside in the summer sun. That brightened it considerably, but the Belgian lace flowers were still quite droopy. I decided to give them a quick kiss with a hot iron. Oops! Tulle and heat don't mix. The flowers survived, but the netting didn't. When the smoke cleared, my vintage veil had a hole the size of a tennis ball.

What have I done? I took a deep breath and tried not to panic. Every one of my mother's mantras came flooding back: "It's not time to worry yet." "Where there's a will, there's a way." None of them helped. And then I flashed back to the spring of 1962 when my 3 sisters and I signed up to dance in the spring recital. Our weekly lessons at Kotchetovsky School of Dance included ballet, tap, character and jazz. We needed four costumes apiece for a grand total of 16 to grace the stage with the other students.

In her typical accommodating manner, Momma agreed to make them. I watched her pin the gold lame fabric to the delicate pattern pieces. It was tedious work. Sitting with her legs in a V, she appeared to be "in the zone" as she cut along the lines with those heavy duty pinking shears.

Over the years, she and that old Singer sewing machine produced plenty of skirts and blouses for school, but these costumes were different. These were for the stage. Momma loved theatre, having starred in many college plays herself. She had no trouble giving up her acting role for motherhood, but she still loved the limelight. Preparing her children for it was a pleasure.

Totally focused on her mission, she didn't notice her two year old, Cecilia, approaching. Naked as a jaybird, she escaped the sister who was supposed to be bathing her and ran across the living room floor toward her mother. Just short of Momma's outstretched arms, the little one stopped and "tinkled" all over the fabric. Momma was speechless for a long moment, and then she put her face in her hands and shook her head like she couldn't believe her own eyes.

Then she calmly got up, went to the kitchen for a roll of paper towels and mopped up the puddle of urine that had ruined an entire evening of work. There were no tears; there were no words. She simply gathered up the soaked material, walked out the back door and threw it into the garbage can.

The next day, while we were at school, she drove to the fabric store and bought more. Somehow, all our costumes were finished on time. A case of the flu kept Momma home from the performance, but the show went on and the four dancing daughters went on with it. We wore tutus for the ballet number, tie-dyed leotards for tap dancing, and skirts with colored ribbons for the Russian chorus line. We wore that gold lame in the finale.

That little trip down memory lane was what I needed to regain my perspective. A damaged wedding veil was not the end of the world. If my mother could recover from her setback with so little drama, I should be able to do the same. I was suddenly certain I could make that veil wedding worthy once again. If not, I knew where to find someone who could.

# NATURE NEVER FAILS

Nature speaks to me. It always has. Maybe that's because I prefer life in the great outdoors. My siblings and I weren't allowed to stay inside during the summer when we were growing up. There was no television at our house until after dark and video games were yet to be invented.

We spent time most every day swimming and reading, but most of our summer vacation was used up on the sidewalks and streets of our urban neighborhood. Our parents encouraged us to stay outside no matter how high the mercury climbed. I probably complained about it at the time. Now I'm glad they did.

My best friend lived in a neighborhood teeming with huge oak trees. Lillie, unconventional to her core, invented a game called exploring. We wandered the woods around her home pretending to be Lewis and Clarke. We pretended to live in the wild. Every day brought new adventures.

Today, I connect with nature wherever I am. Watching squirrels dart along the branches of our tallest trees can be just as appealing as resting my eyes on the bronze rocks of New Mexico. Things that grow are especially therapeutic. Doctors said Shelly, my best friend from high school, didn't feel any pain when she collapsed with a brain aneurysm. For her loved ones, the suffering was excruciating. Losing someone without warning is like undergoing surgery without anesthesia. For months, I woke up crying. I prayed to feel her presence and to know she was okay.

Once again, nature spoke. The message came from a Christmas cactus in my kitchen. It had blossoms when I first received it, but they didn't last. For over a year, it sat in the atrium window, drab as dirt and twice as ugly. One morning months after Shelly's funeral, my prayer was answered. I was pouring my first cup of coffee when something colorful caught my eye. The cactus was covered in red blooms. So many had sprouted overnight, I did a double take. That was my sign that she was okay. Shelly was a flower fanatic.

When my brother-in-law was diagnosed with liver cancer, botanicals came into play again. In his last week of life, Bryan's wife and I planted flowers in their garden. We didn't need his assistance. He didn't have the strength to help even if he had wanted to, but we cherished his presence and occasional comments while we dug. He rested in a hammock under a tree with his Boston Terrier asleep on his chest. Bryan never had children so that dog meant everything to him. As usual, I had no idea how our time in the garden would help me heal. Now I thank God for it every time he crosses my mind.

One of the Cannas that we didn't have room for came home with me. I put it in a pot on our deck and fed it regularly. For the longest time, it generated nothing but green leaves. One morning, I looked outside. It had sprouted a flower unlike the others. Red and yellow streaks of color gave it a unique look. Like Bryan, it was one of a kind. Just like he did, it made me smile.

Last week my next door neighbor called. "Come quick! The birds are hatching". A humming bird had built her nest just outside Gina's bedroom window. Having watched the construction, she set her video camera on a tripod in hopes of capturing the births on film. Like something from National Geographic, we watched the tiny beaks tap their way into the world. Gina had her kids in mind when she set everything up, but it turned out to be just what I needed. Nature's healing power never fails.

What is it about new life that fills me with hope? What is it about hope that always heals? Over and over, nature gives me exactly what I need. Hope and healing are everywhere in nature. They are in the sleek, sharp angles of a burnt orange rock, in the bloom of an unexpected flower, and in the birth of a tiny hummingbird. All we have to do is look.

# NO PLACE LIKE HOME
# DURING GOLDEN YEARS

I have a confession to make. I've been spying on Momma. At 88, she isn't as self sufficient as she used to be. I had concerns about how she was getting along, so I invited myself for a visit. She used to talk about moving out of her house and into a retirement place. "I will know when the time is right," she said. The facility she had her eye on offers daily Mass, an active social calendar and beautiful grounds. Daddy lived there for a short time while he underwent occupational therapy. She knows the place well.

Her friend Patty moved into an assisted living community a couple of years ago. Another friend with whom she worked in real estate also found her way to communal living. After visiting her friends, she has had good things to say about their "new digs".

Last night I visited with an elderly lady who also moved from her big house into a retirement community. She loves every moment of her new life. She and her fellow tenants play cards and go shopping, have happy hours and eat meals together. This lady's eyes lit up when she talked about it. "I have plenty of privacy, but whenever I want company, friends are just a few steps away."

Where do I sign up? It sounded like my freshman year at college. My two Cajun roommates and I were delighted to walk a few hundred feet from our dorm to the cafeteria where we ate whatever they served even if we weren't sure exactly what it was. It was my first experience with mystery meat, but I didn't care. At our house, being late for dinner meant missing out entirely. Dorm life and cafeteria food was Heaven for me. I could embrace that style of living again.

Not Momma. She has decided to stay right where she is. Inside that brick house with drafty windows, she has painted canvases, stitched quilts, and sewed countless costumes and clothes for her kids. Every wall sports a color she selected. To say she has invested herself in it is like saying Martha Stewart is somewhat creative.

Momma and Daddy bought the two-story traditional in the early fifties when they only had six kids. A few years later, a Hispanic couple expressed interest in buying the house next door. Because their skin wasn't white, the listing agent didn't encourage their interest. In fact, the neighborhood deed restrictions said "whites only".

Daddy was furious over the exclusivity. "Mr. Garcia can fight for our country, but not live on our street?" He and Momma went to work on changing the outmoded deed restrictions. Mr. and Mrs. Garcia have lived there ever since. In fact, he was the first to come running when Daddy collapsed in the front yard with a massive stroke. The next week, Mr. Garcia was up on a ladder installing a light at Momma's back door. She wouldn't be driving home from the hospital into an unlit driveway if he had anything to say about it.

I relived so many memories the week I stayed with Momma. Eavesdropping on her life taught me plenty. The bottom line is that she is doing okay. She still dresses herself. She still manages the stairs on her own. Thanks to our brother who lives in the converted garage, she eats roasted chicken and sautéed shrimp on a regular basis. She is healthy.

Is she forgetful? Absolutely, but then again, so am I. During our week together, we took turns misplacing things. I forgot where I put my lap top, she forgot what she did with her key. The bottom line is that she is happy. She still tells a good story and is ready to laugh at all times. She has begun to show her age, but her friends have been doing that for years.

The question still stands. Will she have to move out of her home at some point? Nobody knows what tomorrow will bring. Life in the golden years is even more uncertain. For today, she is able to stay. That's all we really need to know.

## NOTHIN' SAYS LOVIN' LIKE SWEETS FROM MOMMA'S OVEN

"**W**hen are you coming home?"

Those were the first words out of her mouth when I called Momma last week. She hadn't sounded that peppy in months. Her recent lack of energy had something to do with her blood pressure. It now appears that she and her doctor have gotten her back on a healthy track. I could tell by the lilt of her voice that she was feeling better.

After a 3 hour drive, I got to see the improvement for myself. She met me at her back door with a twinkly-eyed smile. Her happiness was another good sign. However, the biggest clue that Momma was herself again was sitting smack dab in the middle of the dining room table. The proof that all was well with Momma was the oversized tin full of cookies.

When we were little, Momma preferred rewiring lamps and upholstering furniture to cooking. While she had dinner ready every day by 4pm, it was never, by her own admission, a very inspired offering. She cooked things like meat patties and broiled chicken, but she left elaborate recipes to the Martha Stewarts of the world. She sewed and painted with wild abandon, but she never acquired a taste for cooking. It had to be one of her happiest moments when she discovered that her fourth child, Mary, had an aptitude for culinary arts. Momma handed over the family spatula to her twelve-year-old and she never looked back.

However, she never gave up her electric mixer. Whipping up sweets for her family continues to be one of her favorite pastimes. Over the years, banana bread and applesauce cakes have brought in money for the church bazaar and filled gift baskets at Christmas time. As delicious as these baked goods are, none rival the popularity of her pecan "icebox" cookies. We call them "Mamaw Cookies" since it was Mamaw Phelan who made them first. With simple ingredients that are always on hand, Momma continues the tradition.

On the first day, the batter is blended and rolled into logs that are refrigerated overnight. The next day they are sliced into silver dollar medallions and baked for exactly 8 minutes. Not 6 minutes. Not 9 minutes, but 8 minutes on the dot. Momma can always tell the difference.

At that point, they are cooled and subsequently added to the large canister in the dining room. That is where most of her visitors come for tea. Those "in the know" make a bee line for the can as soon as they come in the front door. It doesn't matter whether I'm on my way to dinner or even if I have just finished a huge meal, I always reach for one of those cookies. Forget Jello. There's always room for "Mamaw Cookies". Their sugar content places them somewhere between a biscuit and a shortbread. Whatever else they are, they are definitely addictive. I ate about 3 dozen this past weekend.

When granddaughter number 16 got married last year, she made a special request. "Could Gran make Mamaw cookies for the reception?" asked Claire. With a little help from her 9 daughters, Momma cranked out 120 dozen. Then we bagged them in cellophane, tied them with festive ribbons and handed them out as wedding favors.

Baking for loved ones is like singing a lullaby. We sing to soothe our little ones, but it can't help but make us feel better, too. Momma bakes every Thursday to fill the canister for the weekend. Those who come for Saturday afternoon tea party make a big dent in the stash. That's the way she likes it.

With fourteen kids, 35 grandkids, 18 great grandkids, and dozens of in-laws, Momma has lots of reasons to keep preheating the oven. No matter how often she makes them, those cookies are her way of loving an ever growing family. Here's hoping she will keep filling that canister for a long time.

# OPEN LETTER TO YOUNG
# MARRIED COUPLES

Today is our 35th wedding anniversary! As I started writing, my fingers typed 35 tears instead of 35 years. There is something telling in that typo. Every couple suffers tough times along the road of married life. I've heard it said that hardships are stones that sharpen the tools of marriage. Without them, we'd be dull, dull, extremely dull!

That sounds like a rationalization, but it's true. Moving through marriage is like getting past the moguls on an icy ski slope. If you focus on each individual mound, those bumps will take you down every time. The key is to keep your eye on the big picture.

Google says only twenty percent of us make it to our 35th anniversary. Yes, marriage is complicated and yes, it can be challenging. But when it works, it's fantastic. Coming home to my best friend everyday is a gift I wouldn't trade for anything.

That's how I feel today, but our marriage hasn't always been like it is now. The first years were good. When the kids were little, we had a blast. Then adolescence came along and we hit the "squeeze". For us, that meant parenting three hormonally charged children. We didn't recognize it at the time but our children were great. Jimmy and I were the ones with the problem. We couldn't seem to find the balance between feeding the marriage and feeding the kids. It seemed like all we ever talked about was *their* curfew, *their* grades, and *their* ball games. It was not a good way to grow a marriage.

Our difficulties made me wonder how people keep it together during life's demanding times. How did some couples make marriage look easy, fun even? Out of frustration, I asked a few seasoned couples for advice. They were surprisingly eager to share their stories. Tales of inspiration came from every direction. There was so much encouragement flowing, I decided to put it down in a book.

The result was *Texas Twosomes Married for Life*. It's a collection of stories from couples (some names are recognizable, others are not) who survived hard times with their love for each other and humor still intact. Here are a few quotes that I found inspirational.

"You do what you have to do and you pray over the rest"…Wilhelmina Delco

"Harmonize, just harmonize"…Luka Milas

"Don't try to change anybody to fit what you want them to be"…Edith Royal

"You gotta try to live that promise"…Luke Scamardo

"Throughout your marriage, you have to keep choosing to love that person"…Marianne Staubach

Last weekend we drove to east Texas where our family has a "camp" in the woods. In the country, neighbors take care of each other. Within the first hours of our visit, we met a lady down the lane who lent us her lawnmower. Hanging over the fence of her well tended garden, she and I chatted like old friends. She spoke of her recent divorce. They split after 43 years.

I was shocked to hear of it. "Retirement got the better of us," she said as if it was the most natural thing in the world to walk away after four decades of togetherness. What really happened? Did you see it coming? Does he have a girlfriend? I had a million questions, but I didn't ask any. If borrowing lawn equipment from someone you barely know is pushing it, then probing for details about her personal life crosses the line completely. If I had known her during her crisis, I would have handed her a copy of the book. After all, it wasn't my wisdom, it came from veterans. Their stories were vastly different, but the couples had a lot in common. Seven things in particular kept popping up.

1. Humor—They laughed loudly and often.
2. Faith—They shared a strong belief.
3. Forgiveness—They knew how to apologize.
4. Interaction—They spent quality time together.
5. Play—They had fun.
6. Commitment—They chose to love each other every day.
7. Communication—They listened to each other.

People say advice is worth what you pay for it, but I don't agree. The free counsel offered to me by the twosomes was worth its weight in gold. I will never forget those words of wisdom because I've written them on index cards and placed them on my desk. My plan is to keep doing at least one of those 7 things every day. Thirty five years of togetherness feels pretty good. I think I'll aim for sixty.

# PAINTING REVEALS TRUE COLORS

I love hand-me-downs.

Recently, my sister gave us a pine hutch. While the well made wooden cabinet didn't make the cut for her new home, it fit perfectly in our dining room. After a coat of fresh coat of paint, that is. I knew I could make that happen even though the piece was big and had lots of nooks and crannies. My husband worried that I was biting off more than I could chew.

"Let's hire a painter," he said.

"I can do it," I said.

Painting is not new to me. When I was growing up, the family budget didn't cover remodeling. Whenever Momma wanted to make the house look fresh and new, we painted. Changing wall colors was a cheap way to redecorate since she had plenty of free labor in the form of her fourteen children. We could modify the entire downstairs in a single afternoon. One of my favorite old pictures is of me and my sister Carol doing that very thing. Up to our teenaged elbows in satin latex, we are holding our paint rollers aloft like trophies. Our smiles say it all. We are having fun.

I still had some of that youthful enthusiasm, I guess. I woke at 6:30 a.m. on the day of the project, excited about my trip to Home Depot. Having decided on red, I was delighted to find the perfect shade among Glidden's extensive offerings. Called *Red Delicious*, it was the same hue as our leather couch. That was easy. After a minute in the shaking machine, the salesman tilted the paint can my way. "How does that look?"

It looked more like *Hot Pink* than *Red Delicious*. I shrieked, "Yikes! Is that what I picked out?"

"Don't worry," he said. "It gets darker as it dries. You will like it. Customers never believe me, but it's true."

It was a pivotal moment. Standing at the counter of that busy paint department, I remembered something that I had blocked out. While I'm pretty good at applying paint, I stink at picking out colors. Once I selected a shade that looked Pepto Bismol pink after the painter covered the walls of our dining room with it. On the sample, it looked restful and soothing. It was one big "oops" after finding its way to the walls. Those color swatches never tell the whole story.

Desperate to believe the paint expert, I lugged the bag of paint, paint brushes and nylon gloves back home. When I walked through the door and laid eyes on it, the same cabinet that I couldn't wait to get my hands on at the crack of dawn had morphed into a tower of dreaded drawers and shelves. It suddenly had more corners and crevices than I could count. By the time I finished the first panel, my hand was cramping. Shocking red paint was dripping everywhere. Somehow, even with gloves on, my skin was covered in the stuff.

I went inside looking for that picture of Carol and me. I needed to be reminded that painting was fun. Walking back into the house, I must have looked pretty pathetic. The next thing I knew my husband was painting, too. He was willing to help even though

CBS coverage of the last day of The Master's golf tournament was about to begin. He was willing to help even though the leader board showed a three way tie. Most impressive of all, he was willing to help without saying what he was thinking: *I told you this paint job would be way too big.*

No wonder Carol and I looked so happy in that old photograph. Painting with a partner can make all the difference. We were exhausted by the time we finished, but I counted my blessings. He had not mentioned the outlandish color.

The next day we did what one does upon finishing a project. We stood side by side in front of the cabinet, admiring our handiwork. The salesman had been right. Hot pink had turned into *Red Delicious*. I was speechless, but my husband wasn't.

"It was way too much work," he said, "but at least you picked a nice color".

# PATIENCE COMES WITH PRACTICE

I have a confession to make. I am not patient. I am not even sure that I want to be patient. Moving fast is fun. I enjoy getting places and doing things quickly and efficiently. They say that admitting you have a problem is the first step toward recovery. Okay I'll admit it. My name is Donia and I am a *Rusher*.

Conveniently, I married a guy with the same character flaw. We have made a comfortable life together avoiding crowded restaurants and newly released movies like the plague. We are committed to thick and thin and better or worse, but waiting in line was not something either of us signed up for.

When we started our family, we tried to continue the fast pace. Our first two were accommodating. However, when our daughter came along, she put her foot down. She let us know early on that she didn't approve of all the rushing about. Instead of constantly operating on fast forward, her package came equipped with a pause button.

Obviously, she was sent to teach us something. At the age of three, she began showing us how to stop and smell the roses. Only in her case, it was stop and study the blackbirds. Every time we went outside, she found her way to the flock that congregated under the pear tree on our front lawn. After watching from a distance for a few minutes, she gathered her courage and chased them. She clapped her little hands and squealed with glee when they took flight.

Her sense of wonder was delightful, but I had groceries to buy and appointments to keep. Couldn't she commune with the birds from a distance? Couldn't she marvel at the Monarch butterflies from her car seat in the back of our suburban?

I wish I could say that her slow-moving, "present in the moment" ways inspired me to make a change. The truth is that I remained ignorant of my own disorder for years. I just kept rushing her along as if it was part of a responsible parenting plan. It was my goal of checking things off my to do list that got me out of bed every morning. Theoretically, I loved the concept of slowing down and paying more attention. But in reality, when I leaned over to smell the roses all I saw was a plant that needed pruning.

Not surprisingly, I can trace that *hurrying* gene back to my ancestry. My elderly mother still runs up and down the stairs a dozen times a day. When she fell down the front porch steps last week, I suggested she might want to think about moving a bit more slowly. She looked at me as if I had three heads. "Why in the world would I do that?" she asked.

It's understandable. Our world doesn't encourage waiting. Instant gratification is the name of the game. If our internet provider takes more than a few seconds to serve something up, I call the help desk. If the line at the grocery store goes too slowly, I move to another. It's time I admitted I have a problem and that I am powerless over my need for speed. Maybe you have the hurrying gene, too. Here are some questions that might help you discern.

Do you move so quickly that you sometimes hurt yourself? Do you rush around in places where it's inappropriate, like church or hospitals. Do old folks and little children flinch when you approach? If the answer to any of these questions is yes, then you may have a problem. You just might be a *Rusher*, too.

My moment of truth happened recently, when I was waiting for a doctor's report that seemed to take forever. Without any power to make things happen faster, I complained. The medical system moves slowly. Everybody knows that. Then why was I griping to anyone and everyone who would listen? Because I have no patience, that's why. The thing is, I didn't like how I sounded. That's when I decided to grow some patience.

Here is what I have learned since that time. Patience requires more than just waiting. It requires waiting well. Waiting peacefully without complaint; that's real patience. Wearing a smile and a pleasant attitude while waiting is patience at its very best. Checking things off of a daily "to- do" list is no longer my primary focus. Patience is my heart's desire. Now I get to practice.

# PEACE LOVE AND SANDY FEET

My daughter and I are very different. She likes to take it slow and easy. I move fast with one eye on the clock. She thinks things through while I play them by ear. I am all about action and doing. She is into study and contemplation. Even our taste is contradictory. She is into colorful, patterned dresses while I prefer separates and solids.

Even as a little girl, she made it clear she would be doing things her own way. Many of my attempts to influence her ended in frustration. Recently, when we started planning a mother-daughter beach vacation, I vowed to keep my expectations realistic.

We have shared family time in the sand before, but not for just the two of us. Our plan involved a three day trip to celebrate my birthday. I couldn't imagine a better present as we loaded the car with hats, bathing suits, paperbacks and sun screen, and headed south on I-35. Stopping at the grocery store, we agreed on imported beer and veggie chips. It felt like a good start.

As we unpacked at the beach house, there were dark clouds looming. So what? We had plenty of catching up to do and good conversation doesn't require good weather. The next morning, as we sat in rocking chairs on the front porch watching lightening flash across the sky, we did our best to maintain enthusiasm. "This is exciting," I said in a loud voice. It was a challenge to make myself heard over the American flag flapping against the side of the porch. We promised ourselves that we would not allow the elements to interfere with our good time. As soon as we did, the sun came out and burned all the menacing clouds away.

Hallellejuh! I could hardly wait for the next day to dawn. My favorite thing to do at the beach is wake up early to sit in the shallow surf first thing. I love to splash my feet around in the water and scribble my feelings on to the pages of my journal before the pastel colors leave the morning sky.

As I was dragging a plastic chair and beach bag down to the water's edge, my daughter was up at the house turning on the television and coffee maker. She likes to start her day knowing what's happening in the world. To me, having the TV on first thing in the morning is like fingernails on a blackboard. I'll take the roar of the waves for breakfast every time.

Like most girls in their twenties, she likes to tan. While she stretched out on a towel in her swimsuit, I hid my skin under an oversized hat and T shirt, shorts and sunglasses. When it got too hot for both of us, we scampered into the surf (me and all my layers). We took turns riding the waves on a borrowed boogie board. We've always been able to talk to each other, but on this trip, we took it to another level. There was something about standing in waves up to our necks that brought out the honesty in both of us. Or maybe I just realized that we were two grown women having fun and no mothering was required. Our conversation flowed with a carefree openness. To me, it felt remarkable.

When we tired of the salt water, I wanted a bike ride, but she was dying to shop. So we rented a couple of 3 speeds and rode them to various shops along the way. After that, we were too exhausted to dine out, so we ordered fish tacos from a nearby restaurant. We ate them on the beach house's upper deck and watched the sky turn colors as the sun went down.

Finishing my last bite, I looked forward to a quiet evening with my mystery novel. "It's our last night, she suggested. "Let's walk the beach." So we stuck our toes in the sand one more time. Now I can say this from experience. There is nothing like digging for sand dollars by the light of the moon.

In all my visits to the Texas coast, the beach has never looked so good. A vehicle cleaned the seaweed away every morning. There was no sign of jellyfish anywhere. We could see our feet in waist high water. The conditions were optimal, but the mother daughter bonding is what I will always treasure.

My daughter and I will probably always see many things from different points of view. However, we are also beginning to agree on quite a bit. Our priorities start with God and family runs a close second. Both of us put a high value on serenity and we both adore the beach. Peace, love and sandy feet? That's more than enough for me.

# PEACE SETS TONE FOR CHRISTMAS

Let there be peace on earth and let it begin with me. Recognize that Christmas song? Even if I have forgotten the rest of it, that line is familiar. Sadly, there are times during the holidays when the lyrics to that song are my only experience with tranquility. The frantic pace of the season steals my peace faster than anything else. And yet, enjoying Christmas without peace is like trying to do errands without gas in my car. It's impossible. This time of year brings out the crazy in me.

Case in point. Yesterday I went shopping for my husband's gift. Realizing how late it was, I tried a shortcut. As soon as I turned off the main road, a voice in my head said, "Don't do it!" It was a loud voice. I knew I should listen, but I had already made up my mind to be stupid. Have you ever done that? Have you ever known you are about to do something dumb, but you don't even try to stop yourself? Ten minutes into that shortcut, I hit a dead end. What is it about human nature that makes us act so stubborn?

And what is it about biting off more than we can chew at Christmas time that looks appealing? One of my friends buys presents for every member of her family. There are 30 of them. She buys some of them several presents apiece. Even if she starts in July, which she does, she's still buying gifts on Christmas Eve. I don't know how she does it.

One good thing about growing up in a big family is that we're not even tempted to buy a gift for everyone. When we gather on Christmas Eve at Momma's, everybody brings something edible for the dinner table. That is the Caspersen version of a gift exchange.

Somehow, I still manage to freak out in the weeks leading up to December 25th. This morning, I walked into the kitchen and started to toast some pecans for the neighbors. Reaching for the canisters in the living room cabinets, I noticed our half-decorated Christmas tree. I better finish the tree I thought and took a few steps toward a box of ornaments sitting on the table. And then as I reached for a glittered angel, I spotted my car keys beside it. "Maybe I should run to the mall right now", I thought as I glanced at the time, "before traffic gets worse."

See what I mean? I was a holiday chicken with her head cut off. Round and round, back and forth I went with absolutely no direction at all. I ended up organizing my office files. Huh? Seven seasonal things on my to-do list and I spent the morning making my desk neat? It was as if I was traveling on cruise control and somehow got pointed in the wrong direction. By lunch time, I hadn't finished one yuletide task. What in the world was wrong with me?

I lost my peace, that's what. I traded it for the immediate gratification of accomplishing something. That sure doesn't bring peace. There is only one way to quiet my spirit when I start to spiral out of control and it's called sitting still. How ironic that we listen to songs about peace on the car radio while fighting other drivers for a parking space. Like Alice in Wonderland says: "The hurrier I go, the behinder I get."

Sitting still calms my spirit. Ironically, it also helps me get things done. If only I would remember that. If you are interested, it helps to start small. Light a candle and set a timer for 10 minutes. Then clear your mind. That's what I've been told to do. In reality, it doesn't work for me. I found it impossible to focus on nothing.

So I imagine a deserted beach and the rhythm of the waves. For me, that's the essence of tranquility. Some people know it as meditation, but to me that word is intimidating. Sitting still sounds easier. The practice is hard enough without giving it a fancy name.

Like maintenance for the car that drives me around town, peace can carry me through the holidays. Your path to peace might be shorter than you think. Try sitting still. What do you have to lose? The gift of serenity could be waiting for you under a half-decorated Christmas tree.

# PRIDE GOES BEFORE A FALL

Nine screws and a plate. That's what it took to put me back together after my "shoulder plant" last Wednesday. I was riding along on my trusty bicycle, enjoying the wind in my face when it happened. I was traveling a path that I ride almost every day. Like most accidents, it happened in the blink of an eye. One minute I was flying along and the next minute I wasn't.

Obviously I had lost control. Finding myself sprawled on the sidewalk with my bent up bike lying nearby was my first clue. But I was not sure how it happened. The only thing I was sure about was that something on my body was broken. My arm was hanging limp as if it was just barely attached.

In all my years of outdoor fun and competition, I have never broken a bone. However, I've had my share of scrapes and bruises. Cyclists get used to sliding and spilling. Road rash is easy to trat. Until this, the worst of my bike wrecks were handled with ice packs, Neosporin and oversized band-aids.

But this was different. With the help of a stranger who saw me go down, I retrieved my cell phone from the backpack and called for help. My husband was on the scene within minutes. We spent several hours traveling from minor emergency clinic to hospital to an orthopedic surgeon's office. He looked at my x-ray and said surgery was my only option. "Surgery? I shrieked. "Don't collarbones heal by themselves?"

My sister Cindy broke hers 4 times before kindergarten. She had this affinity for jumping off the dresser. All she ever got was a sling. I mentioned this to the doctor and he added insult to injury. Apparently, when "mature" bone fractures into several pieces, it takes more than time and a cotton sling to get it back into place.

In any case, Dr. Moore had room on his surgery schedule the next day. The good news is that he put me back together with 9 screws and a four inch metal plate. The bad news is that Propylol, better known as "Jackson juice" is what they used to put me under. While I fared better than the famous singer, I did not emerge unscathed. Climbing back to consciousness in the recovery room, it felt like someone had scraped my left eye.

The pain was so intense, we drove directly from the hospital to the opthmalogist. He determined that, while it felt like a sharp instrument, the only thing in my eye was a bad scratch. I had done it to myself as a reaction to the anesthetic. He fit me with a protective lens, handed me a bottle of eye drops and sent us on our way. By that time, my husband, who had shown the patience of Job over the past two days, was thoroughly worn out. I was crabby, too. Both of us were at our wits' ends. The difference was that I was on pain medication. He wasn't.

Maybe the lesson I am meant to learn here is that, no matter how fast I am able to go, the time has come for me to slow down. As I look at the Frankenstein stitches on my shoulder, I am not tempted to get back on my bike anytime soon. In fact, just walking by it in the garage makes me nervous. On the other hand, memories fade and time heals wounds. I'm sure I will feel differently at some point in the future.

So that's the story of how I broke my collarbone. I still don't know what caused my fall. I never saw anything on the path in front of me. Upon loading the bike into the back of his SUV, Jimmy mentioned that the left brake cable wasn't connected to the handlebars. That could have caused the accident, but it also could have happened upon impact. I guess I'll never know. But one thing is clear. I need to slow down. My neighbor's words are ringing in my ear. The week before my wreck, I passed him on my bike while he was stuck in traffic. "Wow!" he told me later. "You were flying!" I could almost feel my head swell, but his words brought up a question. Does pride always go before the fall?

# REBA'S GOT HER BLUE JEANS ON

For a while there, we were worried about my mother-in-law. She had been in and out of the hospital for everything from an insufficiency of vitamin B to complications from congestive heart failure. There was one stretch of time when she didn't even feel like getting out of bed to eat. There were other periods when all she wanted to wear was her blue fuzzy robe.

And then she turned 90. We celebrated her big day with a party complete with streamers, banners and enough chocolate cake to feed an army. The party had a Betty Boop theme. Relatives from three generations showed up to celebrate her milestone. I don't know if it was the party or what, but soon afterward, she started getting dressed again. In fact, she started flipping through stacks of catalogues. She wanted some new blue jeans.

When I first started coming to the Crouch house in 1975, one of the first things I noticed was that my prospective mother-in-law's wardrobe was not that different from my own. Thirty years my senior, she dressed more like me and my peers than her own age group. Always a clothes horse, she enjoyed spending money for that purpose and her husband supported her habit. He was a styler, too. For some middle aged women, it wouldn't have been a good idea to dress trendy, but Reba could pull it off.

One day, a few weeks before Jimmy and I got married, she invited me out for lunch. I didn't realize until after we finished our chicken salad and pulled up to the fancy boutique that we were also going shopping for my wedding trousseau. Thanks to Reba and a very helpful saleslady, my wardrobe improved by one thousand percent that day. Every year since, for birthday and Christmas presents she has surprised me with something to wear.

There is this black ¾ length T-shirt, bejeweled with turquoise all around the neckline that wins me compliments every time I have it on. Her selections have never disappointed. Except for once. She gave me a blouse that I didn't like at all. I didn't like the fabric, the color or the style. I couldn't figure out how an item like that ended up with my name on it. It absolutely was not her taste or mine. Later she confessed that the saleslady had talked her into it. That made sense.

Back to Reba and her desire for denim. Right after her 90th birthday party, she wanted blue jeans so she asked her other daughter in law (the one who lived down the street) to pick out an assortment of jeans, charge them to her and bring them home. When her son, Jimmy and I came to visit, she couldn't wait to try them on for us. It seemed like she got younger with every pull of the zipper.

First, she wriggled into cuffed Capris. After that, she tried on Levi 4 pocket Traditionals. All in all, she tried on at least half a dozen pair. After zipping them up, she turned from one side to the other in front of her bedroom mirror. Finally, she was ready for a male's perspective. She rolled her walker into the living room to show her firstborn son. "Are they too tight? she asked. "Does it seem like I'm trying to look too young?"

Jimmy and I looked at each other and burst out laughing. The recipient of two hip replacements, two revisions, a stint, and too many hospital stays to count, this "five foot 2 inch, eyes of blue" lady looked as sassy in her denim jeans as a teenager on the cover of *Seventeen* magazine. Wearing a lime green T shirt and Crocs, she looked ready for another celebration.

I'm not sure, but it might have been more fun helping her into all those blue jeans that day than it was shopping all over town for my wedding trousseau 34 years ago. What fun we had helping her decide which ones looked the best! Reba's got her blue jeans on. May I say she has never looked better?

# REVERSING ROLES FOR HOLIDAYS

Every Christmas, my husband and I pack up a carload of bags and presents and head east. We visit both our mothers' homes for Christmas. Since my husband's mother lives 90 miles down the highway from mine, we manage to celebrate with both. We attend my family's Christmas Eve party. Christmas morning we jump in the car and drive ninety miles for lunch at Reba's house, no sweat. Actually, it takes a lot of sweat, but most of the perspiring happens before we ever set foot in the car.

Our holidays have always been spent on the road. For us that meant arguments and highway fighting. Having grown up amidst chaos myself, I've always felt at home with conflict. The downside to travel besides stress and discomfort included making sure the presents arrived with wrapping and tags still intact.

The hardest part of our seasonal travel is not having a reliable place to stay. Our lodging has always depended on which family member had room. Would it be Momma's spare bedroom? Or if my sister Elizabeth's sons were skiing with their father, maybe we'd bunk up in Kyle's room. Worst case scenario, we could always stay at the La Quinta 6 blocks away. It wasn't ideal but, to me, it seemed worth the inconvenience to be with my side of the family for Christmas.

One year, my husband talked me into staying home. This won't be so bad, I thought. We'll start a few traditions of our own. On Christmas morning of 1990, I pulled out Momma's cornbread recipe. It was time to make my first turkey dinner.

I set the table as if the king of England were coming. If we were starting traditions, I was determined to do it up right. Then I undercooked the turkey and overcooked the rolls. Disappointment loomed over the table like an uninvited guest. Oddly, it had nothing to do with the food. There simply weren't enough people around the table. Ten minutes after we sat down, the kids (they were 5, 8 and 9) started fidgeting. There is something wrong with a meal that takes 3 hours to fix and fifteen minutes to eat.

The next year, we re-embraced our holiday travel plan. Fast forward twenty years and we have a totally different situation. Our daughter lives in Houston, so the rest of us hang out at her place. Last year, she gave Jimmy and me her comfy bed with clean sheets still warm from the dryer. There was a pot of chili simmering on the back burner when we came through her door. She made us coffee both mornings of our stay and taught me the art of dipping pretzels and popcorn into dark chocolate. It's my new holiday favorite!

There is nothing quite as wonderful as switching roles with your kids. Eating their food, sleeping in their beds, and reading their books. It's heaven. When our children started reciprocating, it took me by surprise. Mothers are programmed to nurture. I guess we get out of practice at receiving tender loving care from others.

Having tasted my daughter's offering, I believe I could get used to this.

Here's something extra: our daughter cooks. Yesterday, she made Pizzelles- paper thin, cheddar cheese crackers. Delicate as snowflakes, they are baked in a waffle iron and melt on your tongue. Our girl learned how to make them from her Cajun mother-in-law. The surprises just keep coming.

Our last night at her house, I heard her clanging pans in the kitchen. "Mom, how long should I bake the peanut blossoms?" she called. "Eight minutes," I called back. I started to get up, but then realized she didn't need me. And, as Martha Stewart says, that's a good thing.

Parenting calls for getting our kids ready. We help them gather up their gifts and then point them toward the world. It's meant to happen gradually, but some of us have trouble letting go and that prolongs the process. Some kids live with their parents until they're thirty. We know this firsthand. I now believe that it really doesn't matter how long it takes to launch kids. As long as, at some point, they learn to care for themselves. The icing on the cake comes when they take care of us.

# REVIVING ART OF LETTER WRITING

How long has it been since you got a letter? I'm not talking about a thank-you note or an invitation to something. I am referring to an old fashioned *"Dear Donia, How are you doing?"* complete with a stamp and a postmark. It's been ages since I got one, but that may be about to change. I'm on a mission to resurrect the art of letter writing. It will probably take some effort. I have a feeling that there aren't a lot of people out there whose heart skips a beat at the sight of a hand written letter.

On the other hand, there must be other hopeless romantics like me. Whenever I find a piece of personal correspondence mixed in with my junk mail and bills, I get excited. In fact, I'm getting pumped just thinking about it. Maybe I can get this pen pal thing off the ground if I start with my mother.

During my freshman year in college, she kept in close touch. In fact, I received more than a few lovely letters that year. My sister, Mary, sent regular updates. She will never know how much her letters helped me cope with homesickness. If not for her generous checks I couldn't have joined my roomies for Sunday lunch at the Italian restaurant near campus. Mary's support, moral as well as financial was truly remarkable.

I also got letters from Uncle Howard. He was the only sibling of my paternal grandmother. Grandmother

Caspersen remains a mystery to her grandchildren. She left this world suddenly and tragically before Momma and Daddy ever met. The only information that trickled down to the grandkids was that she was beautiful, ambitious and greatly misunderstood.

Since Daddy wouldn't talk about his mother, her mysterious persona grew. Which is why, when her only brother wrote to me in Baton Rouge, I wrote him right back. In addition to being curious about my heritage, I was intrigued with the idea of getting mail from the west coast. At the time, Uncle Howard was our only relative in California. I wanted to find out everything I could about him and his late sister.

But then, disapproving aunts discouraged our long distance relationship. Were they afraid he would paint their mother/his sister in an unfavorable light? All I know is that I felt guilty about writing, so I stopped. In any case, our short-lived connection taught me something. I will never again miss an opportunity to climb out on the limb of a family tree. Letters can be invaluable; especially when they are all that connects people like me and Uncle Howard.

Letters are also important to lovers. Lots of couples separated by WWII depended on letters to keep their love alive. Our only uncle on Momma's side, Uncle Bubba used them to get his courtship with Aunt Natalie off the ground. It was 1943. He was a flight instructor at the school where they trained army pilots. Aunt Natalie was a new waitress in the mess hall. At first, he called her on the phone every day. Then she moved with her parents to a house in the country and they didn't have a phone. That's when he switched over to letters. However, unlike the rest of us, he did not rely on the post office.

He did get a little help from his students. As his "pilot in training" flew low over Aunt Natalie's house, Uncle Bubba dropped his tenderly worded love letters. Some were lost in the fields, but a few landed near the house. One actually floated onto her front porch. Decades later, she showed me one of them.

Like fine wine, letters from loved ones get better over time. I'd give anything to have held onto that correspondence from Uncle Howard. I regret that, but there are ways I can make it up to myself. I could start trading letters with other Caspersen offspring like cousin Barbie in Chicago or cousin Joan in San Francisco. Maybe they know something about Uncle Howard. Or even better, maybe they have a clue about our mysterious matriarch.

Swapping letters with cousins could help me understand my father's reticence to share. At the very least, I would get to know them better. One thing's for sure. Getting letters would make my life better no matter which friend or family they come from.

# SEEING WITH EYES OF THE HEART

For years, I enjoyed perfect vision. As a little girl, riding along with a carful of siblings, I was the one who could read street signs from a block away. Navigating fell to me long before I got my license. "Nope, this isn't where we turn," I said as Kathy clicked on the blinker.

Eight of my siblings and both parents have worn glasses as far back as I can remember. One of my sisters wore lenses so thick, they looked like the bottoms of old fashioned coke bottles. Another one's cornea was scratched in a childhood accident. To this day, only one of her eyes sees clearly. Growing up with siblings who had to keep up with glasses reminded me how much simpler my life was.

On the other hand, when tinted contacts came into vogue, I was jealous. That was my first experience with the green eyed monster. One day, our younger sister, Elizabeth came home with eyes the color of a blue topaz. Having been fitted with colored contacts earlier that day, she looked like a cover girl. I was desperate for eyes that shade. One evening, when I should have been doing algebra homework, I popped one of Cindy's lenses out of its case and into my eye. And then, of course, I couldn't get it out. It wasn't until hours later that her boyfriend, Mike finally managed to extricate it from my bloodshot eyeball. That was the end of my envy.

My vision was 20/20 until a few years ago. I began to notice that words and numbers were getting fuzzy. "Cheaters" from the drugstore enabled me to read books and menus, but did nothing for the numbers displayed on the big screen TV during Texas Ranger baseball games. I couldn't tell what inning the game was in or how many balls and strikes the pitcher had thrown. After much denial, I found my way to an ophthalmologist's office. He sat me down in his examination room and asked a few questions. I admitted I had never been to an eye doctor before.

"At your age?" he said. My face fell. So did his. I'm quite sure he wished he hadn't blurted that out to a woman on the other side of fifty. His faux pas was embarrassing, but I got over it when I realized how much clearer the world could look through his lenses. I had had perfect vision up until recently and now, thanks to my new glasses, I have it again.

I love my new specs. They bring clarity, confidence, and a bit of cosmetic help as they are the same shade of green as my eyes. At some point, everyone needs help to see. It's one of the side effects of "maturing". Yesterday, while pulling up nut grass in hundred degree heat, I stopped to clean the sweat from my glasses and made peace with my failing eyesight one more time.

Recently, my siblings and I held a meeting to talk about Momma. At 88, her eyesight and reflexes are both failing. Her doctor has recommended that she quit driving. Not everyone in the family agreed with the idea. Some felt the measure drastic and premature. After all, she hasn't had a wreck or a ticket. "Won't taking away her car be the same as taking her freedom?

And so the discussion went. Getting thirteen people to agree on anything is difficult, but when everyone is passionate about the subject matter, it's really hard. All of us had Momma's best interest at heart. We just didn't agree on what that was.

As I left our gathering, I noticed that everyone in the family wears glasses As our collective eyesight fades, it's a perfect time to open the eyes of our hearts. That's a good kind of irony, don't you think? Given the choice, I'd rather see the world through my heart, anyway. Our eyes have been known to deceive us. Our hearts rarely do.

# SERVING OTHERS SERVES US BEST

L ast night was girl's night out. Our monthly get-togethers started out as happy hours in restaurants. Lately we have been doing dinner in each other's homes. Everybody brings something and the hostess cooks up the entree. Last night Joan made pot roast.

There is something about serving each other that makes the evening better. We linger longer while sitting around one of our own tables after the plates are cleared than we ever would in an eating establishment. That's because, like the hospitality, the conversation is kicked up a notch. Last night, while catching up on various family members, our talking touched on why some people live longer.

Could longevity be related to generosity? Cathy's grandmother died last year at the age of 103. She managed to live independently until after she hit the century mark. Cathy said that when she was a young working girl, she made daily trips to the hospital where her stepmother (think Cinderella's stepmom) was dying. Apparently, the old woman had been so unkind to so many, no one else would visit her. At the end of a long workday, Mimi took a bus to the hospital to sit beside someone who had been especially unkind to her.

My mother is almost 89. She also epitomizes the servant's heart. Perhaps that can be said for anyone who raised 14 children while running a real estate business.

Upon retiring, she accepted a volunteer position at her church: coordinating lunches for the geriatric community. For almost twenty years she ran the program called Daytimers, so named for members of the church who no longer drive at night. She joked about serving salad and quiche to ladies ten years younger.

Now she makes quilts for newborns. Watching her stitch fabric squares into colorful patterns, these words flood my memory: "Idle hands are the devil's workshop." That was her mantra when we were growing up. She seems to think her longevity is a result of staying active. I thinks it's a by-product of her oversized heart.

As last night's table talk affirmed, it isn't just moms who put others first. Anne and Joan's dad will turn 90 in a month. Having run a working cattle ranch and raised 13 kids, this man has gotten damn good at giving. Over the years, chronic back pain has made everything, even walking, difficult. Yet when his oldest daughter competed in a local horse show, he was there to see her win a ribbon.

Today I ran into friends who had been married for 65 years. He is older, but she is the one who was hospitalized recently. At 93, he was her primary caregiver after her surgery. Their children check in with them often, but mostly these two take care of each other. When one of the grandkids got married in Miami last spring, Nana watched from the first pew. I asked them about raising 5 kids. Each gave the other all the credit. I rest my case.

Of course, my theory about the connection between big hearts and long lives is based strictly on anecdotal evidence. You may be thinking, at this very moment, of a self- absorbed person who lived well into her golden years. Once we lived next door to an elderly lady who gave that same impression. She seemed selfish. I'm embarrassed to admit that I had already made an unfair judgment before learning that she and her husband were big supporters of a local children's home. A generous heart is not always obvious.

Experts say stay active. Exercise the body and the mind. These tips seem obvious, but sometimes staying fit doesn't lead to longevity. While pondering this topic, I read an article that featured 82-year-old Supreme Court Justice Sandra Day O'Connor. Her advice? "Keep doing things that matter".

Serving others matters.

# SHELLY LIVES IN OUR HEARTS

We just got back from a wedding in San Francisco. The groom was the eldest son of my best friend, Shelly. She was not in attendance. She died more than a year ago, well before her time. I worried that her absence, a ragged hole in the family fabric, would affect the festivities. I should have known better.

Shelly and I bonded in Sister Mary Ellen's ninth grade classroom sharing miniskirts and makeup. During our teen years, I spent more Friday nights at her house than my own. When I ran short of funds in my last semester at the University of Texas, I thought I'd have to quit school and get a full time job. Shelly, my roommate at the time, wouldn't hear of it. She called her parents. They loaned me the money and the two of us finished college together.

While I have known her first born child since he was in the womb, I didn't meet Patricia, the bride-to-be, until recently. We stood together in Shelly's hospital room trying to wrap our brains around the fact there was no hope for her recovery. Standing in a circle around the hospital bed, we held hands and prayed. While we didn't get the answer we prayed for, I'm guessing the young couple's love for each other turned a corner that day.

A few months later, they announced their engagement. I marked my calendar and booked a flight as fast as I could whip out my credit card. These kids are family. I was excited about witnessing the beginning of their new journey. It wasn't until I started packing for the trip and thinking about the fact that Shelly wouldn't be there that something new came over me. I had been sad for a long time, but now I felt something else. Anger! The mother of the groom should be there for such a momentous occasion!

Then I remembered what the hospital chaplain said on Shelly's last day. "As much as she helped you while she was on earth," he said, "she will help you all the more from Heaven". Father Mike gave Shelly her final blessing and then stood beside us while we told her goodbye. His words had a powerful punch. They offered hope where there had been none. I clung to those words of comfort as I left the hospital. Apparently, I had forgotten them.

The wedding couldn't have been more glorious. The rehearsal dinner was al fresco. We feasted our appetites on salmon and veggies while feasting our eyes on the Pacific Ocean. Strung with lights from one end to the other, Bay Bridge twinkled against the midnight blue sky. We raised our glasses and spoke of how much we loved the beautiful bride and groom.

Soon after Shelly went to Heaven, her first granddaughter came to earth. This wedding weekend was Kate Michelle's social debut. I carried her around the party showing off her polka dot dress and red tights. Rare is the person who isn't moved by an infant's smile. The child has her father's eyes, that's for sure. But there was something about the way she worked that party that made me think of Shelly.

My favorite moment happened during the exchange of vows. The couple grabbed hands and faced each other all ready for the minster's big question. Do you take Patricia as your lawful wedded wife to have and to hold from this day forward until death do you part? In a loud voice with a big smile, he proclaimed: I *absolutely* do!

His adlib made us laugh. The added adjective sounded familiar. It sounded like Shelly. She *absolutely* spoke in superlatives.

I must admit, the wedding weekend was wonderful. While Shelly was not there in the flesh, she could not have been more present in Spirit. For the first time in a very long time, thinking about her did not cause me to sob. I wasn't the only one who came back from the wedding inspired. The texts from family members started rolling in before we even unpacked.

Helen Keller said, "The best and most beautiful things in the world cannot be seen, nor touched … but are felt in the heart." That's where Shelly lives now. In our hearts. We carry her with us wherever we go. And sometimes, like her son's wedding weekend, she carries us.

# SOMEBODY HAS TO COOK!

I got married in the dark ages.

Back in the old days, wives were expected to cook. My grandmother did it, my mother did it, and every one of my aunts did it. While Jimmy and I didn't discuss the division of labor before exchanging vows, we managed to carve out an extremely traditional marriage. It must have been understood that we would follow the marriage model our parents had built. As birds of a feather, we have been "flocking together" for 36 years now. For the most part, he maintains the cars and yard while I manage laundry and meals. So far, it seems to be working.

During our courtship, the chef's hat was still up for grabs. He tried to woo me with his mother's famous Crayfish Etouffe recipe. After inviting me over for dinner, he served up a dish so loaded with cayenne pepper, I couldn't choke down more than a bite of it. In spite of his culinary miss, I felt pressured to cook for him. My mother, all too aware of my under-developed kitchen skills, suggested that I keep it simple.

"You know, you can't go wrong with rib eye steaks," she said. Then she suggested a red wine marinade. Not knowing the difference, I soaked those beautiful cuts of grade A meat in a bowl of red wine vinegar all afternoon. By the time I pulled them from the oven, they were tougher than shoe leather. They looked like it, too. That night, love was truly blind. His taste buds must have been handicapped as well because the man ate everything on his plate as well as mine.

I guess I won the job of chief cook by default. Jimmy settled happily into the role of dishwasher. With a bottle of 409, my husband can put the shine back in a kitchen faster than anyone I've ever known. Our close friends love it when we come to their homes for dinner. He's a busboy on steroids. He is perfectly happy with his role as am I. As you can see, we complement each other well.

Our son and daughter-in-law have adopted a different style. Whether cooking or cleaning, they share it all. He chops vegetables while she tears lettuce for the salad. He cooks sausage for the pizza while she spreads cheese on the dough. Their apartment kitchen is small, but they never run into each other. In fact, they move with the grace of Astaire and Rogers. It's inspiring.

I love feeding family. There is something about filling the stomachs of loved ones that makes me feel satisfied, too. Does that sound old-fashioned? I'm okay with that. I've learned that gathering loved ones around the table is basic to the care and feeding of all relationships. Families do less dining at home these days, but cooking is one thing that will never go out of style. It doesn't matter who wears the chef's hat, but somebody has to cook.

# SOMETIMES OUR KIDS TEACH US

For the past many months, we've have been planning a wedding. My daughter and I have bought a dress, booked a venue and a church, hired a caterer, ordered a cake, and put down so many deposits, I have lost track. All that is left is the fun part: opening presents and being toasted by friends and family. The hard part is over. Or so we thought.

When the engaged couple came to town for the holidays, he said he had been experiencing chronic pain. It started in his back. Before long, he felt numbness in his legs. The test results showed a mass at the base of his spine. In a few short days, he went from a hard-working 28 year old who couldn't wait to get married to a cancer patient confined to a hospital bed. His future was filled with uncertainty.

Over the next few weeks, more tumors showed up. Clearly, the cancer was aggressive. The doctor recommended postponing the wedding. As the bride's parents, we embraced that idea. Their future was uncertain enough, wasn't it? But the young people had the opposite reaction. They wanted to get married as soon as they could.

So they switched their venue from church to hospital. In three days the wedding plan was completely transformed. The guest list shrunk from 200 guests to immediate family as that's all we could fit in his room on the 12th floor of MD Anderson. I was full of fear. This appeared to be an impossible way to start a marriage. I spoke my mind which prompted our daughter to speak from her heart. "What do the wedding vows say?" she asked. She had loved this man for 6 years. It was time to give the bride away. It was time to trust our daughter.

In spite of the setting or maybe because of it, the ceremony was unforgettable. The groom spoke his promises from a prone position. The bride stood beside him in a long, lacy gown, clutching white roses with one hand and holding his with the other. They promised to love one another through sickness and health. The effect of those words was not lost on anyone.

It has now been thirty days since the wedding. He was transferred from the 12th to the 10th floor for chemo treatment. Then he was discharged and received chemo as an outpatient. When his platelet count sank to a scary low, he was rushed to the emergency room for a blood transfusion. That was followed by more platelets. Finally, he was readmitted. His new wife was with him every step of the way. These days, she sleeps in a recliner beside his bed, getting about two hours of shut eye at a time. The life they lead is heartbreaking, but they are together. They wouldn't have it any other way.

Living in a different city, her calls are our life line. I drop everything when I see her name flash across the top of my cell phone. Before answering, I breathe a silent prayer. *May it be good news.* There isn't any except that our new son-in-law's positive attitude is rubbing off on our daughter. "*Today he got out of bed for a ride in a wheel chair,*" she said brightly.

*"We went up to the atrium where we looked out over the city."*

*"This morning, he stood by himself."*

Small victories, they call them. I call them miracles because that's what it must take to carry them through the day. Having left their jobs in another state, these twenty-something kids have signed on for full-time employment of a different nature. He spends his days fighting a monstrous disease. Hers is to walk beside him every difficult step of the way. They've been man and wife for less than a month, but their marriage has generated a lifetime of inspiration. Sometimes our children teach us. This is one of those times.

# STILL KISSING AND MAKING UP

I used to think that couples either stopped arguing or got divorced by their third decade. Clearly, that's not the case. Jimmy and I have been together longer than that and we are still fine tuning our relationship. This morning, I did something that irritated him so much that he told me to "Mind my own business!"

It was bad enough that he said those words to me, much worse that he said them in front of his mother. I don't remember what I said in response, but I'm certain it was not my finest moment. His mother sat transfixed during the shouting match, her blue eyes big as saucers. We lobbed a few verbal volleyballs back and forth. And then I stormed out of the room.

Moments before the blow-up, I was telling his mom what a great man he was. He had served me a cup of coffee exactly the way I like it- with warmed almond milk. One minute we were smiling and happy and the next, we were at each other's throats. What happened?

I think I know. In the middle of our morning coffee, Jimmy answered his phone and left the table. When he came back, I asked, "Who was that?" That's all it took to get the fireworks started. I was so angry, I laced up my Nikes and hit the streets. I raced up and down the sidewalks like a woman possessed. Stretching my legs and pumping my arms has been known to take the edge off my fury. However, in the meantime, I look a little crazy. In fact, if I saw a woman in spandex and a floppy hat shaking her head and cussing her way down the sidewalk, I would probably cross to the other side of the street.

After 36 years, our arguments are as predictable as hundred degree heat in August and equally oppressive. In the middle of my power walk, the light bulb went on. Last year, I left my teaching job to try my hand at freelance writing. Since then, I have been writing columns at the kitchen table. Meanwhile Jimmy, who has run his brokering business from home for years, negotiates real estate in the office not fifty feet from me. After a decade of leaving the house at the crack of dawn and not returning until dinnertime, I'm suddenly in his space all day long. Asking him who was on the phone reminded him of that.

Obviously, it's just as much my house as his, so I don't need his permission to work at home. Still, establishing some ground rules ahead of time would have been a good idea. Not discussing changes and transitions beforehand is like attempting natural childbirth without Lamaze classes. So what can I do to help him reclaim his tranquility?

I could keep my questions to myself until the end of the day. He has never been much for socializing during business hours. He wears a game face from 8 to 5. It used to hurt my feelings that he doesn't call me during the day, but not anymore. We both like our space. With my nosy question, I had stepped over a line.

When I returned from my walk, he was standing in the driveway. I could see from a distance he was waving an olive branch. "I'm sorry", he said. "Me, too", I answered. "I'll try not to be so nosy," I added. He grinned. "That would be nice." We both laughed.

My husband and I still have conflicts. There is nothing wrong with that. An occasional blowup is the best way to clear the air. Believing that we will ever get to a place of permanent peace is a fantasy. Instead of viewing fights as failures, perhaps I should see them as sparring matches that keep us healthy and in good shape. Without arguments there would be no kissing and making up. And isn't that the best part of all?

# TAYLOR MADE FOR
# COUNTING BLESSINGS

It's the last Thursday of November. All over the country, fellow Americans are gathering around tables. The tradition began with the Pilgrims at Plymouth Rock when they thanked the Native Americans for helping them get settled in their new land. In similar fashion, families take time before gobbling up turkey to say special thanks to God for the things He has provided us. At our house, we make a point of stating the blessing for which we are most grateful. As I pondered my richest gifts, I couldn't help but think of our late son-in-law, Taylor.

Our daughter brought him home to meet us in the fall of 2008. Ever heard the expression: Hail Fellow Well Met? That was Taylor. He was loved by one and all. We were lucky to celebrate several holidays with him over the six years we knew him. He brought plenty to our table every time. I am not just talking about the green bean casserole.

In one way, Taylor was more like his father-in-law than either of our natural born sons. Intrigued by mechanical challenges, he knew how to fix things and was eager to do so. Patience was the sharpest tool in his toolbox. Last year over the Thanksgiving weekend, he spent hours untangling Christmas lights from the boxes in the attic. Then he braved the rickety ladder to hang them along our roof line. All that time, he never let on about his dizzying fear of heights.

I will never forget the first weekend he came to stay with us. It was late July and our air conditioner was acting up. The thermostat in the living room read 85 degrees. "Want me to take a look at it?" he asked. I just looked at him. Surely, he was kidding. That was before I knew he had technical talents. "Seriously," he pressed. "It could be something surprisingly simple." The problem called for a simple adjustment to the compressor. Voila! The house was once again inhabitable.

We were delighted when he asked for our daughter's hand and had fun helping to plan their big white wedding. Then, out of the blue, Taylor began to experience disabling back pain. By the time the diagnosis was confirmed, the cancer had spread. The burning question on everyone's mind was the same. Why?

Ironically, Taylor was the one to come up with an answer. "God has a plan," he said. We hated that response and took turns telling him. To this day, I don't know how he managed to fight the disease with everything he had and, at the same time, accept it. Let's just say that he taught us plenty during his 3 month battle. It was always about keeping faith.

I'll probably always wonder why Taylor died so young, but I have no doubt about his life's purpose. A natural optimist, he was destined to teach us how to keep on believing. He also reminded us to count our blessings. A "glass half-full" kind of person, he lived that way long before the sarcoma showed up. No matter how dark the cloud, Taylor found the silver lining.

It was a big funeral. The church was filled with mourners from every point in his twenty nine years. On his website, there were posts from people as far away as New Zealand. His 7th grade English teacher said he was her favorite student. College peers told stories of generosity that his wife, sister and parents had never heard before. He wasn't a saint and he would not appreciate any attempt to make him sound like one. We're talking about love here, not sanctity.

He married our daughter after being diagnosed and died forty days later. We didn't get much time with him, but the impression he made on us will last forever. And while he was at it, he taught us something about trusting God's plan.

This year, there will be an empty chair at our Thanksgiving table. We miss our son-in-law. He made us all a little better. For that we are grateful.

# TOGETHERNESS MEANS OVERDOING IT

Do you hear that? It's the sound of silence. The last of our family members have headed back home. The kitchen is clean and beds are stripped. There is a load in the washing machine. This is the first time I have sat down in three days. Easter weekend is over and I'm exhausted.

It's always this way. Easter is the only holiday we have always celebrated at home. Instead of taking it easy and keeping things low key, I tend to overdo it. The first holiday in our Austin house, Momma and Daddy drove over from Houston. We hadn't gotten around to hanging curtains yet. As soon as my parents got settled in the guest room, Momma suggested we do something about that so we ran down to Hancock fabric. Our plan, crazy as it sounds, was to cut the fabric out on Friday night, sew the drapes on Saturday and hang them that evening.

Three children under the age of 7, an elaborate meal to shop for and cook, and baskets to fill, so why not make a few curtains while we're at it. Momma told me about a style that called for minimal sewing. "We don't even have to hem them," she said in that convincing tone of hers. "We'll just "puddle? the fabric on the floor."

"Puddle" has never sounded appealing before, but if it's Momma's recommendation, it must be a good one. The clerk at the store was a tougher sell. I will never forget the look on his face when Momma started "guesstimating" our wall measurements. I let her do the talking. After all, she had made curtains for every room in her house. As the salesman stretched and cut yard after yard of polished cotton, I had second, even third thoughts. *Maybe we should forget the curtains and concentrate on Easter eggs.*

But we didn't. Momma was right. We turned that polished cotton into window coverings in no time. Honestly, they didn't look all that great when we finished, but it didn't matter. We were already on to the next project: filling Easter baskets.

There is an unwritten rule at our house. Everybody gets a basket no matter how old or young. Filling Daddy's basket for Easter of 1987 proved to be especially gratifying. He died of a stroke a few months later. I treasure the video showing our three kids directing their grandfather in his search for his hidden basket. "You're getting warm, Papaw." The kids had never seen their 72-year-old grandfather that excited about anything before. He still had on his pajamas as he searched high and low for his basket of chocolate bunnies.

Daddy lives in Heaven now, but Momma still comes for Easter weekend. And we're still cramming way too much into the weekend. This year we baked two turkeys, a cake, and a green bean casserole. Because there was no room in the oven, a skillet full of brussel sprouts had to be grilled on the BBQ pit. All of that was done before Mass on Sunday morning.

At one point, there were six of us sidestepping each other in the kitchen. My six months pregnant daughter-in-law and 89-year-old mother were working like pack mules to get food on the holiday table? What is wrong with this picture?

In our family, we aren't happy unless we are working. Then we complain because we're exhausted. As I thought back to the homemade icing Momma whipped up for our Easter cake, I felt guilty for a minute. Then I remembered she taught me everything I know about the art of overdoing.

By this time next year, our grandchild will be about 9 months old. Our hands will be full with the happy task of caring for him. Note to self: there will be no curtains and no cake. Today I will call and thank all family members who contributed to our jam-packed Easter weekend. I will follow that with a well-intended promise. Next year, all our eggs are going into one basket: the baby.

# VOTING HONORS SOLDIERS

Some say it's our duty. Others declare it a privilege. Whatever you call it, casting a ballot is the single best way to get your voice heard. Whether Democratic, Republican or Libertarian in America, we all have one thing in common. We have the right to vote. Our soldiers have preserved that right for us. Thanks to them, we still live in the land of the free and the home of the brave.

However, peace and freedom come with a price. Countless men and women have paid that price. Perhaps you have a niece serving in Afghanistan or a grandfather who fought in Vietnam. Some soldiers come back from the battlefield scarred by their experience. Others do not come back at all. My father-in-law was a POW for 22 months. Here is his story.

James William Crouch Jr. was a bombardier pilot in the United States Air Force. Stationed in London, he and his unit flew air raids over Germany. In the spring of 1943, upon returning from a mission to bomb an aircraft assembly plant, he was shot down. Seconds before his B-17 crashed, he buckled his parachute and ejected from the aircraft. With a leg full of shrapnel, he sought help from a sympathetic Belgian woman. She bandaged his wounds. She gave him clean clothes.

She helped him elude the Germans who were searching every house in the vicinity. But when the

Belgian woman's husband, a Nazi sympathizer, found James in his house, he turned him in. Following his capture, the Nazi soldiers forced a doctor to dig the shrapnel out of his leg and then relocated him to Stalag Luft III. He was imprisoned there for almost two years.

He and his fellow officers were liberated from the hell hole just south of Berlin by Patton himself. Recovering from pneumonia, he returned to his hometown of Port Arthur, Texas. That's where he met and married the love of his life. His story had a happy ending, but toxic memories haunted him for years.

He couldn't share his experience with anyone for decades. It was his grandson who finally got him talking. Will's 5th grade history class had just started studying WWII. "Will you come to my school and tell us about it, Papaw?"

I grabbed the video camera and drove my father-in-law to Valley View Elementary school. Our family hero stood in front of that elementary schoolroom and relived his war story for the better part of an hour. He cleared his throat so many times, I thought he might be having an allergic reaction. I was about to turn off the camera when I realized he was choking back tears. "After all this time", he told me, "I still get emotional about my crew members. Especially the ones who didn't come back."

The kids listened wide-eyed as he painted the picture of oppression that was life inside that German camp. They were fascinated by the system the prisoners used to dig escape tunnels from the barracks to the barbed wire fences. Students weren't the only ones hanging on his every word. The teacher and I were riveted. We had merely watched the movie, *The Great Escape.* James had lived it. He died two short years after recording that classroom video. How we treasure that VHS tape!

We have heroes on my side of the family, too. My father served in WWII. As a naval lieutenant, he followed orders on an aircraft carrier in the Pacific. My uncle flew B-17s over the Himalayas. My older brother was stationed stateside during his tour of duty, but he would have gone wherever his orders dictated. Real soldiers are like that. They obey. They sacrifice. They serve.

Many of us will vote next Tuesday because we want our voices to be heard. It is our right because soldiers defended that right. That is a fact. We honor our loved ones by remembering their contributions. We honor them even more when we vote.

# WAITING FOR MY TURN
# WITH MOMMA

I grew up crowded.

Living in a house with 13 brothers and sisters didn't offer much individual space. Not to mention the lack of peace and quiet. Even the homework hour was noisy. I remember sitting at the table, surrounded by siblings and books. We discussed our teenage heart throbs in between math problems. Solitude was as rare as second helpings in our house. There were people in every room.

Recently, it was just Momma and me in her house. I had driven over to see her for the weekend and somehow, we ended up spending Saturday night by ourselves. It was quite unusual. For the entire evening, neither of our phones rang. No one knocked on the front door. In the comfort of that old house and well-worn dining table, Momma and I shared a pork roast with a side of stories. Listening to her talk about days gone by, I thought back to another time and place. There was only one time during my entire childhood when I had my mother all to myself.

It was a beautiful, "blue sky and sunshine" kind of day in the spring of 1956. Momma drove up to the curb outside my Kindergarten schoolroom. As I walked down the sidewalk toward the station wagon, I looked in the back seats for my younger siblings. Carol, Judy, Steve, Colleen and baby Kevin were nowhere to be seen. Settling into the front seat, I turned to my mother.

"Where is everybody?"

She said they were at home with a babysitter. "We are having lunch by ourselves," she informed me. My heart leaped with joy. I can't recall what either of us ate or wore, but I remember exactly how I felt that day. Like an only child. I'll never forget the day I didn't have to share my mother.

In spite of how pitiful that may sound, life in a big family was positive for me. I would not trade anything for it. Brothers and sisters were always there for me. There was always someone to help straighten out the tangles in my hair and my life. Sixth from the top, I benefited from Kathy's, Candy's, Cas', Mary's and Cindy's vast experience.

All that interdependency left an impression on my soul. We still love being together. Just last month, we gathered in Chicago for the wedding of one of my nieces. Momma doesn't travel as much as she used to, but she'd have to be on her deathbed to miss a family wedding. We took turns escorting her around the windy city.

The art of sharing was mastered early at our house. It was our first lesson. Nine sisters and I shared a bathroom, a couple of closets and one chest of drawers that held bras, socks and underwear. If you think that selecting undergarments from a communal set of brassieres doesn't bond sisters for life, think again.

It's been awhile since we shared bedroom space or clothing, but we are still taking turns with Momma. At 87, she is not thrilled about losing the freedoms that old age steals. Giving up her driver's license and losing her short term memory have been sheer torture. On a positive note, the slower pace of her twilight years makes it easier for us to catch up with her.

As a result, her calendar stays full. Steve comes by for coffee during the week. Candy brings her granddaughter over for afternoon tea. Kathy stops on her way home from the produce market and Cecilia and Elizabeth drive over for visits after work. Kevin is temporarily staying in one of her spare bedrooms. Carol makes dinner for her on Sunday evenings.

Cas, who lives in her garage apartment, is in and out all day long. Lots has changed, but one thing hasn't. We're all still trying to get time with Momma. The question is will we drive her crazy in the process? These days, she is more interested in the answer to a different question: What was I thinking when I had so many children?

She laughs when she says it. I hope she's kidding, but it will take more than that to run me off. Not expecting another "table for two" anytime soon, I will patiently wait for my turn with Momma. I've gotten pretty good at sharing.

# WORDS OR WEEDS? NO CONTEST

Every April, I get this overpowering urge to grow things. We inherited a well- landscaped yard. The previous owner planted lots of bulbs, so every spring flowers appear as if by magic. Suddenly, purple irises and bright red daffodils are visible through the window of my kitchen door. As soon as I see them, I want more.

Sometimes I fantasize about digging a vegetable garden. Last weekend, I bought a tomato plant. With fingers crossed, I hauled it from my car to the backyard and plunked it down in the sunniest spot I could find. It already had fruit hanging off of it when I saw it in the store. "Oh good", I said. "All I have to do is keep it growing".

That sounds easy until I think about how many plants have died on my watch. If only I had my sister's skills. Cindy's thumb is as green as the ferns that dot her flower beds. Everything she plants flourishes. She's so committed to the earth, she has two gardens. One is full of brightly colored flowers and blooming bushes while the other one produces lettuce, cucumber, and squash.

Cindy is happiest when she's digging. She even thinks about gardening while on vacation. One summer, she snagged lemons from a tree in Tuscany and then smuggled them past the customs agents. Ultimately, she planted the citrus seeds in her backyard. As soon as they got home, she and her husband had a good story to go with the photos from their European trip. It's been a few years and now they also have an Italian lemon tree growing right outside their kitchen window.

We have a fruit tree in our yard, too. Like the irises and daffodils, our peach tree was here when we moved in. I was thrilled when the tree first exploded in pink flowers. Imagine my delight the morning I discovered those blossoms had turned into fruit. Plucking one from a branch -it was somewhere between the size of a grape and a golf ball- I ran into the house with it. "We have peaches, we have peaches!" I shouted to my husband in the shower. "Come see!" He took his time getting dressed before coming outside. By then he was grinning from ear to ear. Can you tell we are city slickers?

The following year we waited for our harvest with eager anticipation. Those fuzzy green balls appeared right on schedule. What followed was a major disappointment. Each peach had a tiny white worm inside. When I sliced into the first one, the neighbors heard my screams two blocks away. Jimmy got on the phone with the county extension agent to determine how to fight the slimy pests. He sprayed with a natural pesticide, but it was too late for that year's harvest.

Now we are waiting once again. Like a mom with a sleeping newborn, I check the tree often. The produce won't be ready until mid June so I'm still thinking about planting a vegetable garden. I called Cindy for her input. "Gardening is a lot of work," she reminded me. She knows how impulsive I can be. "You really have to *love* it."

"Do I *love* it?" I asked myself. If I'm totally honest, the answer is no. I don't *love* gardening. I *like* gardening, but I *love* writing. If I am asked to choose between putting words on the page and putting seeds in the ground, I'll take paper every time.

Cindy and I are alike in one way. We have found our passions and we feed them daily. It's ridiculous to think that I might invest as much time cultivating and planting as I do writing. There are only so many hours in a day. Not enough time to be a gardener and a writer unless I'm content to be average at both. The next time I yearn for home-grown vegetables, I'll just drive over to Cindy's and ask her for a cucumber. Better yet, I'll write about it.